CAREERS, COLLEAGUES, AND CONFLICTS

SAGE HUMAN SERVICES GUIDES, VOLUME 43

SAGE HUMAN SERVICES GUIDES

a series of books edited by ARMAND LAUFFER and CHARLES D. GARVIN.
Published in cooperation with the University of Michigan School of Social Work and other organizations.

$ A **SAGE** HUMAN SERVICES GUIDE **43**

CAREERS, COLLEAGUES, AND CONFLICTS
Understanding Gender, Race, and Ethnicity in the Workplace

Armand LAUFFER

Published in cooperation with the University of Michigan School of Social Work

SAGE PUBLICATIONS
Beverly Hills   London   New Delhi

For information address:

SAGE Publications, Inc.
275 South Beverly Drive
Beverly Hills, California 90212

SAGE Publications India Pvt. Ltd.
M-32 Market
Greater Kailash I
New Delhi 110 048 India

SAGE Publications Ltd
28 Banner Street
London EC1Y 8QE
England

Printed in the United States of America

Library of Congress Cataloging in Publication Data

Lauffer, Armand.
  Careers, colleagues, and conflicts.

  (Sage human services guide; v. 43)
  1. Psychology, Industrial. 2. Organizational
behavior. I. Title. II. Series: Sage human services
guides; v. 43.
HF5548.8.L286 1985   650.1   85-14276
ISBN 0-8039-2040-7

FIRST PRINTING

CONTENTS

To

Tamar and Yitzchak

Whose Inner Explorations Lead to Unlimited Opportunities

Baruch HaMakom

INTRODUCTION

The book you are about to read is not the one I had intended to write. I set out to do a fairly straightforward demystification of agency personnel practices and procedures. About halfway into the first chapter, two students stopped by for a talk. I was amazed to hear myself accused of racist and gender biases because of some remarks made in class. One does not take such accusations lightly when one teaches in a school of social work. I certainly didn't.

None of us are free of prejudices, and I did some inner searching to bring to the surface whatever it might have been that I had conveyed. It was not a painless process. Nor was it without pain that the two students had approached me. How much of what they had perceived was in me, I wondered, and how much in them?

The next few weeks led me to begin exploration of a wide variety of related issues. These are all reflected in the pages that follow. They deal with culture, ethnicity, personality and conflict in the workplace. They also deal with careers and professionalization, with collegial relationships and with roles and role-conflicts. Writing this book was a struggle. I think reading it will be as well.

In order to write it I had to dig deep inside. I also dug into the literature. And I interviewed dozens of students and practitioners, some of whom you will meet in the book. Their identities are disguised, of course, but perhaps only partially. If you recognize anyone, I hope it will be yourself. In Chapter 1 you will meet Yolanda, Sam, Ali, Millicent, Carl, and Harvey. Don't let yourself be put off by their genders, racial and ethnic backgrounds, social class characteristics or the work they perform at the All-Families Service Center. The place is mythical. The characters are real. They are you and I, and many of the other people you have met at school and at work.

Each chapter focuses on several issues that probe the relationships between people in the workplace. One of the issues we examine is the fit between individual capacities and aspirations and the demands (expectations) placed on them by others on the job or by fellow professionals. Although each chapter is distinct, the issues presented blend into each other and are often dealt with again and again from a different conceptual point of view. Each chapter also includes a set of exercises and a rather extensive bibliography.

The exercises are designed to bring *you* into the book, in effect interacting with Yolanda, Harvey, and the others. They are a guide to self-study and analysis. The suggested readings are intended to provide you with a guide for further intellectual inquiry. They include both classic and contemporary sources. You may be conversant with the classic sources from earlier undergraduate and graduate study. You may be familiar with some of the more contemporary materials from your work in a social agency or from your perusal of the professional literature on occupations, personnel practices, management, burn-out and job stress, gender and ethnicity studies, and so on. But juxtaposed the way they are, these materials should lead you to new understandings and to more effective work-related practices.

Used properly, the book—with its exercises and readings—may help you make more intelligent career decisions. It should also be useful in helping others whom you may counsel or supervise at work.

Two acknowledgments: The first is to Everett Cherington Hughes, who introduced me, and dozens of scholars at universities throughout the world, to the sociology of occupations. The second is to Wyatt Jones, who provided me with guidance and support in my first study of social work students and their career choices. Finally, a word of thanks to Dan Madaj, who typed the manuscript quickly and accurately and with an eye to correcting my errors in grammar and syntax.

Ann Arbor   —Armand Lauffer

Chapter 1

GETTING TURNED ON TO WORK
Satisfaction, Motivation, and Effort on the Job

Clark

Yolanda Stephenson turned off her favorite Motown station just before reaching the freeway exit. Straightening up, she squared her shoulders and shook off the rhythms that had filled her head and energized her body since leaving home. By the time she pulled into the lot behind the All-Families Service Center, she was ready to assume the quiet and professional demeanor she was known by and which she expected of herself in the position of clinical supervisor. The switch in mind-set was not unfamiliar. It was a price Yolanda had long been willing to pay for success in social work, her chosen career, for the esteem and respect she received from her (white) colleagues, and for the security that came with a well-paid, tenured position. As the first member of her family to earn a university degree, she felt some other obligations as well.

* * * * *   *Lebanese*

Samich Faoud Mansouri met Yolanda in the parking lot. They nodded to each other pleasantly but without commitment. "Sam" runs the agency's New Americans Project. As a 19-year-old, Sam had left his native Lebanon because of civil strife but never waivered in his commitment to its victims. He decided early to seek a career opportunity that would enable him to be of service to his countrymen and others in the Chaldean community. To be of service had always been expected of Sam. His father and grandfather before him had both been physicians, tending to Beirut's poor. Shortly after beginning his undergraduate work, Sam switched from premed to a social work major. An encounter with a counselor at the university, herself an MSW, was the deciding factor. He found in her a dedicated, empathic and helpful professional—a role model for his own career. He has never regretted the choice of social work as the profession through which he would seek to achieve his personal and community-related objectives. On completion of his MSW, Sam began employment at the Center. He continued to study, earning a law degree on a part-time basis. Although the clients he serves are not well understood by many of his colleagues at work, he is respected as a competent practitioner, good administrator and effective advocate.

Eventually Sam hopes to establish a nonprofit organization advocating for immigrant rights. But he is in no hurry. His initial sense of urgency has diminished somewhat (not incidentally) following his marriage and the successive arrival of two daughters on whom he dotes.

*   *   *   *   *

Alberta Schmid was already sitting behind her desk in the receptionist's office when Yolanda and Sam walked in. Ali always arrived early in order to get the day's work organized, enjoying the interaction with other staff as they come in. Feeling wanted, knowing she does her job well and being appreciated means a lot to Ali. "Ali knows her job. I don't know where we would be without her," Bill Clapman, the agency's director, has told other staff members more than once. And the word gets back to Ali. She also enjoys the give and take with clients, feeling a sense of deep satisfaction when she routes them properly to Center staff. The job does not pay terribly well, but then Ali's education has not gone beyond two years of junior college. Still, the position is secure, and last year when she unexpectedly needed surgery, the agency's extensive health benefits covered all her expenses. Staff members visited her regularly while she recuperated, letting her know how much she was missed.

*   *   *   *   *

A moment or two later, Millicent arrived. Millicent Kapinski likes to call herself a "retread." After 20 years of teaching in a Catholic parochial school, she came to the conclusion that life within her order was too restrictive. She also found herself in increasing conflict with Church policy. Now, as a family life education specialist, she has discovered a newfound freedom with full opportunity to express her commitments to others. Her age—Millicent at 53 is one of the older staff members at the agency—and her warmth lead others to seek her out as a confidant. "I've become," Millicent admits with a smile, "everybody's 'Polish mother' around here."

* * * * *

Carl Farrell arrived late. "It really doesn't matter," he thought to himself. "Hardly anyone around here is interested in the things I care about." As the agency's accountant, he is somewhat of an outsider in an organization dominated by social workers and allied human service professionals. It's not that Carl's tardiness signifies poor performance. To the contrary, Carl does his work competently, but without enthusiasm. He discovered early that excessive zeal, especially when you deal with budgets, sometimes leads to conflict.

And Carl doesn't like to fight. Using a wry humor to keep people at a distance, he does his best to avoid conflict. But all this leaves Carl isolated socially, and this in turn leads to feelings of depression and of being unproductive, misplaced, and unloved. His energy is low and he often feels that life has somehow begun to pass him by. He just can't seem to connect with the upbeat attitude of other staff at the agency.

People at the Center might be surprised to hear of it, but Carl is a jazz enthusiast, playing one or two nights a week at a club in a nearby suburb. It's not something he shares about himself with the others. Although Carl feels something in common with Millicent, whom he respects for her seriousness, and senses a kinship in spirit with Yolanda . . . both the male-female and Black-white thing, and his own normal reticence to become too close to anyone, lead to his isolation from them as well.

* * * * *

Harvey Marcus chose not to come to the agency that morning. He was on his way to the state capital, where he was scheduled to meet with public welfare officials to go over his latest proposal for a series of innovative community treatment facilities. The juices were flowing. Harv always felt this way when starting the negotiations process of putting together a new package of services. "It's the primitive hunting urge," he once confided to his wife. And it paid off, not only for his agency and its clients, but also in terms of his own career. He had moved rapidly in the five years since completing his MSW—a lot faster than he might have by playing it safe on a clinical assignment within the agency. Harvey thought of himself as being on the "cutting edge" of practice.

He was, in fact, on another sort of cutting edge, operating on the boundary, so to speak, between his agency and the community. One nice thing about being on the boundary was the opportunity it provided to expand the programs for which he was responsible. There was a price to pay, of course. One could get too far ahead, cutting oneself off from one's colleagues as one's programs became severed from the agency's core. But it was a risk worth taking, and the rewards, including rapid advancement in responsibility and income, were great.

* * * * *

You've undoubtedly met Yolanda, Sam, Ali, Millicent, Carl, and Harvey—or others like them—at work or at school. You'll meet them again as you read on. We'll explore why they and others choose to work at the jobs they do, why they've selected careers in the human services and the benefits they derive (or hope to derive) from such work. We'll examine the conditions that contribute to job satisfaction and productivity, personal and professional advancement and the achievement of agency missions. As you read each chapter and complete the exercises within them, you will be able to assess your own situation with all its attendant risks and opportunities. You'll be better able to define what turns you on (and off) about work and your relationship with others. You'll be able to define your career objectives more clearly, and to anticipate pressure and tension points to avoid. Let's begin by examining work and working.

THE MEANING OF WORK AND
WORKING FOR MEANING

The French word for work is *travail*. In English, travail means "trouble," "suffering" or "exhausting labor." The Hebrew word for work is *avodah*, but its translation into English is "service," and the connotation of service is to render one's duty, to give aid, and to be helpful. Somewhere between these two definitions lies the reality of your situation and mine.

When something is working, it is functional and in good order. When people are working, their activities may or may not be functional or in good order. Unlike things, people have reasons for working and feelings about what they do, how they do it and how others respond to it. Those feelings have much to do with whether they consider work to lead to suffering or service. People work in lots of places and at many tasks. They may work at being good parents, at improving their golf games, at beating the stock market, or at their jobs. For our purposes, we're going to focus on *job-related* work—those activities in which people engage in order to gain material necessities and luxuries. But the benefits they derive, or hope to derive, from work are not only material. They are also social and personal—benefits not limited to the workplace but which, if absent or difficult to achieve, may render the place where you work less than satisfying, and the work you do less than meaningful.

People work to meet their security, social and personal objectives. These might be summarized as follows:

(1) Security objectives
   (a) Earning sufficient income, now or in the future.
(2) Social objectives
   (a) Meeting the expectations of others—family members, friends, the society at large (that its "productive" members will be gainfully employed or involved in the service of others).
   (b) Belonging, being accepted, receiving affection, establishing friendships.
   (c) Being appreciated, esteemed for one's contributions, achieving recognition and status with its attendant impact on self-esteem.
(3) Personal objectives
   (a) Self-actualization, achieving one's own potential, growing and developing in response to challenge.

(b) Engaging in service to others, helping people.

(c) Taking responsibility for social or community change, making a difference.

These objectives are not always so clearly stated, nor are they mutually exclusive. Much of the time we pursue several objectives simultaneously without being fully aware of them or of how they serve either as motivators or as criteria by which we assess our satisfaction at work. For each of us, in fact, several of these objectives interact in tandem so that they are not easy to distinguish, one from the other. Moreover, at different stages in our careers or personal lives, one or some combination of these objectives may be dominant. Even the level of intensity with which they affect our behavior and our feelings about our circumstances is likely to change over time. Nevertheless, it is possible to clarify how these objectives affect us and the work we do, just as it is possible to become more sensitive to how they affect others.

Think a moment about what you already know about Yolanda, Sam, Ali, Millicent, Carl, and Harvey. Take a moment to make an educated guess about each of their motivator-satisfiers.

In making your assessments, you probably took into consideration what you know of each person's background, current work responsibilities, and relationships to colleagues at work. Admittedly, your knowledge about others is limited. You probably know a good deal more about yourself and your own situation. Consider **Exercise 1.1** as a warm-up for a somewhat more difficult assessment. In the second exercise,[1] you are asked to take a look both at yourself and your situation, and to make some determinations about what the future may hold.

That exercise may have given you a chance to think. If you are like most people, chances are that the fit between what you are looking for in a position and what a particular job has to offer you is not all that close on all items. Moreover, as you discovered in completing the first exercise, different people have different motivator-satisfiers. It is not likely that any work setting is going to meet everyone's needs or expectations. This doesn't mean that either you or they should settle for something less than satisfactory. To the contrary, the fact that things at work are not fully satisfactory is often the motivator to make them better. Reality factors, of course, sometimes lead us to accept a

1. If you are having difficulty making this assessment in this assignment, turn to the end of this chapter and do **Exercise 1.5** first.

Exercise 1.1

Staff Motivator-Satisfier Assessment

Based on what you know about them, check those items which you think act as important motivator-satisfiers for each of the agency staff members you were introduced to at the beginning of the chapter. Take a moment to reread the vignettes if you need to refresh your memory.

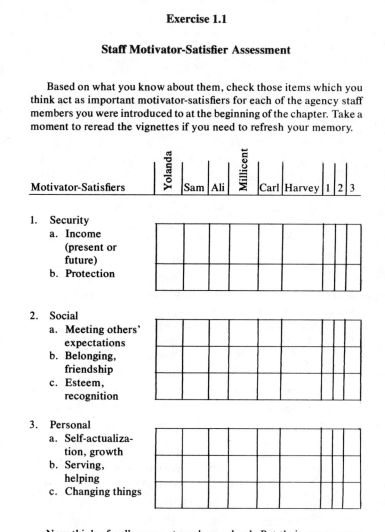

Motivator-Satisfiers	Yolanda	Sam	Ali	Millicent	Carl	Harvey	1	2	3
1. Security									
a. Income (present or future)									
b. Protection									
2. Social									
a. Meeting others' expectations									
b. Belonging, friendship									
c. Esteem, recognition									
3. Personal									
a. Self-actualization, growth									
b. Serving, helping									
c. Changing things									

Now think of colleagues at work or school. Put their names over Columns 1, 2 and 3 and complete the same assessment for them.

situation that may be less than satisfactory. Sometimes the cost of changing something on the job may be greater than the hoped-for benefit, especially if that something to be changed is you—your sense of self, your skills or the tasks you may be required to perform or your aspirations and those of others who are important to you.

USING CONCEPTS TO UNDERSTAND MOTIVATION

We'll explore a number of these issues when we examine the meaning of careers (Chapter 3), your relationship to colleagues, subordinates and superiors (Chapters 2 and 5), job restructuring (Chapter 6), and the meaning of professional practice (Chapter 4). First, however, it may be helpful to examine what others have discovered about job satisfaction, motivation and meeting needs on the job. In doing so, we'll examine some of the findings of the researchers and the ideas of the theorists who are most often referred to in the literature on personnel practices and human resources management.

Exercise 1.2

Personal Motivator-Satisfier Assessment

1. Begin by determining what you are looking for in a job, any job (Column 1). Rate each of the motivator-satisfiers in terms of importance to you at this stage in your career or worklife. Three stars (***) = very important; two stars (**) = important; one star (*) = somewhat important. A blank indicates that this factor is not important to you at all.
2. Now complete the second column. Here you will be assessing the extent to which your current job meets those expectations. Again, use a three-star rating system, with the stars indicating the extent to which the job provides you with each of the motivator-satisfiers (i.e., *** = very much, blank = not at all).
3. In the third column write "OK" where you feel that no adjustment is necessary because columns 1 and 2 match, or because the degree of congruence is acceptable to you. Put a plus (+) in those rows where the fit is not close but where you think some change in your favor is possible, and a minus (−) if you think there is little likelihood that what you are seeking and what the job has to offer can be reconciled.

Motivator-Satisfiers*	(1) What you are looking for in a job	(2) What your** current job has to offer	(3) Adjustment possibilities

1. Security
  a. Income
    (present or
    future)
  b. Protection			

2. Social
  a. Meeting others'
    expectations
  b. Belonging,
    friendship
  c. Esteem,
    recognition			

3. Personal
  a. Self-actualiza-
    tion, growth
  b. Serving,
    helping
  c. Changing things			

* This juxtaposition of terms is taken from Herzberg, discussed later in this chapter.

** If you are not currently employed, think of a job you recently left, or one you are considering as a future possibility.

I want to begin with a warning. There is some danger in limiting our exploration to these theorists. First of all, their ideas are still only tentative and not fully borne out by empirical research. Second, most of what they have written has tended to be accepted uncritically by people responsible for developing and managing personnel practices in many organizations, often with unproductive results. But there are some advantages as well.

Because these are the theorists most often quoted in the literature (and by personnel directors), it is important for you to be familiar with them so as to understand the rationales often used for an agency's employment policies and practices. Such understanding may help you in negotiating more satisfactory working conditions and job benefits. It will help you understand where persons responsible for those policies and practices are coming from, assuming that they are familiar with the same theorists. This is not to suggest that the concepts and theories described in the following pages have neither validity nor potency. To the contrary, they are powerful ideas that can and have been used to create more satisfying work environments based on increased understanding of human behavior at work and the motivations behind that behavior.

Concepts and theories can be used in a pro-active way, leading you to take action on the basis of ideas that have some empirical validity. They can also be used defensively, protecting you from the abuse of others who may be using them incorrectly or selectively against your best interests.

In this chapter we'll examine a number of "need" theories, one at a time, and then explore an expectancy-motivation model that shows some promise of being especially helpful to workers and managers alike. This model draws, to some extent, on the theories discussed earlier.

NEED THEORIES

If you've taken an undergraduate psychology course or delved into any of the personnel literature, you are undoubtedly familiar with the works of the late Abraham Maslow of Brandeis University. In the early 1940s, Maslow, a psychoanalyst and psychotherapist with a penchant for anthropology, attempted to integrate into a single conceptual structure much of what he had learned from analysts like Freud, Adler and Jung, with the work of Carl Rogers, Gordon Allport, Henry Murray, Eric Fromm, and others. He postulated that all persons have a hierarchy of needs. These can be described as follows:

5. Self-Actualization: growth, achieving one's potential, self-fulfillment.

4. Esteem: self-respect, autonomy, sense of competence and a sense of achievement (internal factors); recognition, status, attention, prestige (external factors).

3. Belonging and Affection: acceptance, love, friendship, working cooperatively with others.

2. Security and Safety: protection from emotional and physical harm; shelter, warmth, health and mental health protection.

1. Physiological: drives to satisfy fulfillment of hunger, thirst and reproductive and other bodily needs.

You probably recognize in this hierarchy all of the motivator-satisfiers we included in the two preceding exercises. Maslow further postulated a notion of "prepotency" which suggests that once a person's lower order needs (physiological and security) are satisfied with some degree of consistency, he or she is freed to pursue higher order needs for love, esteem, and self-actualization. Unfortunately, Maslow did not support his ideas with a great deal of empirical research of his own. Nevertheless, his schema had an enormous impact on psychologists and others concerned with motivation in the workplace. There is an almost intuitive logic to his ideas which makes them easy to understand and accept. But some social scientists are skeptical of the intuitive, while others are too easily captivated by it.

For this reason, the 1950s, 1960s, and early 1970s witnessed a spate of research efforts aimed at validating or disproving Maslow's ideas. In a now classic review of those studies, Porter, Lawler and Hackman found that although there is evidence that the activation of higher order needs depends in part on the satisfaction of lower-level needs, the needs for belonging, esteem and self-actualization do not operate in a hierarchical manner. Most people are motivated by and can pursue each of the higher order needs simultaneously. The need for money and security may reduce the readiness to pursue higher order needs, but they too can act as motivators, though they tend to do so only temporarily. Once satisfied, lower level needs no longer motivate. Higher order needs, on the other hand, especially the drive for self-actualization, seem to be insatiable once activated.

In 1972, Clayton Alderfer published research findings that led to consolidating Maslow's hierarchy into three basic needs. His ERG theory combines the two lower level needs into one: *Existence*. *R*elatedness needs include both esteem and belonging, while *G*rowth needs refer to the search to be most fully what one can become. Although all of these can be pursued simultaneously, frustration of one's existence or relatedness needs can lead to at least a temporary reduction in the pursuit of growth needs. Where there is much opportunity for growth and personal development, existence needs may take on less importance. Conversely, where growth needs cannot be satisfied, greater attention may be directed at securing better pay, working conditions and other existence-related benefits.

At about the time of Alderfer's publication, David McClelland was engaged in using the TAT (Thematic Apperception Test), along with follow-up interviews, to study how people project their needs in response to work-related stimuli. The most commonly verbalized themes were the needs for achievement, affiliation and power—needs expressed with different degrees of intensity and frequency by different people. In some cases these were expressions of personality, in others they reflected the challenges and opportunities available at work, and in still others they seemed to be a function of a respondent's life-stage or place on the career ladder.

For example, *n* Ach (need to achieve) might be high for a young manager whose career is at an early stage and for whom many opportunities to demonstrate competence and receive rewards for achievement are available. For those moving up the administrative ladder, *n* Pow (need for power) might take precedence over the need for achievement at the point where a person finds himself or herself in a position of command or with opportunities to affect the direction of the organization or to influence others within it. Those whose opportunities are blocked might redirect their needs toward affiliation and the establishment of good working relationships with colleagues (*n* Aff—need for affiliation).

In subsequent studies, McClelland and his associates found *n* Ach to be a prime motivator for those entrepreneurs involved in starting up small businesses, while the desire to have an impact on others (*n* Pow) was a strong motivator for those moving up in larger and more complex organizations. Some critics of these studies have characterized the use of quasi-mathematical symbols like *n* Ach and *n* Aff as *n* Bam—*the need to bamboozle*. There may be some justification for this observation, since some researchers tend to believe that their findings reflect more than partial truths. This weakness can be detected among those practitioners who latch onto a theory and ride it for all it's worth, and more.

They follow what philosopher Abe Kaplan has called "the Law of the Hammer." In plain English, this law can be stated as follows: "Give a small boy a hammer and he'll find that everything in sight needs pounding."

It would be good to take note of this observation before proceeding. Maslow, Alderfer, and McClelland's contributions to our understanding have been substantial, but they should not be accepted uncritically. Like other concepts from the social sciences, they should be used by practitioners to the extent that they are found helpful as guides to interpretation and understanding but only sometimes as guides to action. They are too tentative and imprecise to direct our practice behaviors in all instances. We are still, most of us, much like the blind man trying to describe the elephant. Each of our observations should be recorded and used where helpful, but we should not fool ourselves into thinking that any one observer's contribution is enough to comprehend the whole.

This caution notwithstanding, it may be useful to examine one more researcher's efforts to identify satisfiers and motivators. Even before Alderfer began his work, Frederick Herzberg conducted a set of interviews with 200 engineers and accountants in the Pittsburgh area in order to test the relationship between lower order needs and the need to grow and develop psychologically. Interviewees were asked to pinpoint those events on the job that led to increased feelings of job satisfaction, and those others that led to increased dissatisfaction.

Herzberg found that the factors leading to satisfaction were associated with the work itself. They included achievement, recognition, responsibility and advancement. These he called "motivators" because when present they seemed to lead to better performance and increased effort. To the extent that these were absent, there was "no satisfaction," and respondents reported lower motivation to achieve.

The second group of factors tended to be focused more on the work *situation* rather than on the work itself. If people complained about work, they tended to cite problems in the work context or environment. These "dissatisfiers" included pay and benefits, relationships with colleagues or supervisors, company policies or rules, job security and tenure. Such items were rarely cited as "satisfiers." Herzberg concluded that these "dissatisfiers" (which he later called hygiene and maintenance factors), when improved, tended to lead only to temporary increases in satisfaction (with the elimination of some dissatisfaction). Thus they cannot be considered to be motivators. A major finding of this two-factor approach is that the many people who are motivated by the satisfaction they derive from their work may have considerable tolerance for poor working conditions—in other words, they can live with some dissatisfaction without it detracting from their satisfaction.

Herzberg's "two-factor" theory has spawned hundreds of similar studies in efforts by researchers and personnel directors to determine what might lead to increased motivation in specific workplaces or within specific occupational groupings. Not everyone can be expected to respond the same way as the engineers and accountants in the 11 Pittsburgh firms studied. For example, many human service workers are likely to include "supervision" and "relationships with colleagues" among their satisfaction factors rather than among their hygiene or dissatisfaction factors. In contrast, studies of blue collar workers indicate that some hygiene factors such as better pay are indeed motivators, especially when the work itself is dull and unrewarding.

You may find the two-factor theory intriguing. I do. But I also find it somewhat limiting. First of all, grouping satisfiers and dissatisfiers into a two-dimensional theory of work satisfaction seems to be a grand oversimplification. Second, it tends to ignore any other theories that might be used to interpret or explain findings. The most telling criticism of Herzberg's work is that he made no effort to relate motivators to actual job performance. In fact, his translation of the word "satisfier" into "motivator" has been criticized by some as naive at best or as sleight of hand at worst. In conducting his interviews, Herzberg asked respondents whether job satisfaction increased their motivation to put greater effort into their work. Most responded affirmatively. But how else could they have answered? Ask most people if they are satisfied at work, and you are not likely to hear them tell you "yes" but that they are also unmotivated!

USING NEED THEORIES ON THE JOB

Clearly, need theories are flawed, yet they can be used heuristically to comprehend our own motivations and to assess the extent to which outcomes we value are achievable on the job. They can also be used in developing greater sensitivity to our colleagues and their motivations, to the needs and interests of those we supervise, those who supervise us, and to the volunteers whom we may recruit and assign to various tasks.

Let's list the theories we've examined:

—Maslow's hierarchy includes the following needs: physiological, security, belonging, esteem and self-actualization.

—Alderfer regrouped these needs into his ERG theory of Existence, Relationships, and Growth.

—McClelland identified the need to achieve (*n* Ach), the need for affiliation (*n* Aff) and the need for power (*n* Pow).

—Herzberg found that satisfiers (which he later called motivators) were of a different order than dissatisfiers (which he called hygiene factors).

Think about what you already know or have surmised about Yolanda, Sam, Ali, Millicent, Carl, and Harvey, and then go on to **Exercise 1.3.**

As your answers to the questions in **Exercise 1.3** may have suggested to you, motivation is explained by a combination of factors that include the work itself, the need for achievement discussed by McClelland and the combination of extrinsic and intrinsic rewards that may be possible within the workplace. The meaning of those rewards, and the extent to which they are likely to serve as motivators, are explored more fully in what has come to be known as the "expectancy model."

THE EXPECTANCY MODEL

Unlike the work of Maslow, Alderfer, McClelland, and Herzberg, the expectancy model does not limit examination of what motivates people (needs or satisfactions). Rather, it places emphasis on the conscious and semiconscious thought processes that lead people to act in certain ways in the workplace. The underlying assumptions of the model are as follows:

Exercise 1.3

Application of Need Theories to Agency Practice

1. Using either Maslow's or Alderfer's formulation, generate as many questions as you can to help you uncover what motivates each of the six staff members to behave as they do on the job.

2. Are there identifiable prices that the staff members must pay to achieve satisfactions and that may serve as de-motivators? What questions would you ask in an effort to find out?

3. How would you get the answer to those questions—by asking the staff members directly, through observation, by asking others (e.g., colleagues and supervisors)? Why did you answer as you did?

4. Does McClelland's addition of *n* Pow add substantially to the questions you would ask? How?

5. Would you ask the questions differently if you were following the approach used by Herzberg? If so, how? If not, why not?

6. Of the four approaches, which do you find most useful? Why?

7. Assume for a moment that you were the agency's personnel director or the person responsible for employing and assigning the six staff members. How would you use this information in your decisions about whom to employ and for what jobs?

8. Think about your own job. To what extent were these questions asked of you? Should they have been asked? To what extent did you seek answers to these questions in determining whether or not you were interested in the job? If you did not, or did so only partially, how might your decision have been affected by more thorough exploration of these issues?

We, each of us, desire particular benefits and rewards for the things we do, and we may have preferences among them.

We also have expectations about whether, in any given situation, the things we do will lead to a particular outcome, including achieving those rewards we value mostly highly.

The model, which I'll describe more fully in a moment, was first articulated by Victor Vroom. It has since been refined and studied extensively by Edward Lawler III. Vroom uses three key concepts in his model: valence, expectancy, and instrumentality. Valence is the extent to which a person values a particular outcome or reward. When you starred the items in Column 1 of **Exercise 1.2** ("What you are looking for in a job"), you were indicating the valence of each of the eight motivator-satisfiers listed.

Expectancy refers to the perceptions a person may have about the probability that a particular circumstance, effort, or action will lead a particular outcome or result. For example, in Column 2 of the exercise, you indicated your expectations about the extent to which your current job can offer you the rewards you seek. In the context of Vroom's expectancy model, you would want to get even more specific. You would indicate your expectations that certain actions or efforts on your part will yield specific outcomes.

The third concept, instrumentality, is what gives the expectancy model its unique character. It refers to the extent to which we believe that a first-level outcome will yield a second-level outcome. For example, you might, as Harvey Marcus does, believe that by "operating on the boundary" you can increase the opportunity to expand programs you are responsible for. Negotiating a contract will enable you to expand the agency's services to a particular client population. By the same token, achieving that outcome may lead to a second-level outcome, thus increasing your personal satisfaction through helping others or changing things. For example, it may also yield rapid advancement and increased income (security needs) and may heighten the esteem with which you are regarded by others in the organization (social needs).

Vroom depicted the model schematically as shown in Figure 1. To a large extent, motivation is directly related to *expectancy* × *valence*. Both are in part the result of an individual's earlier experiences, his or her sense of self (ability, capacity to achieve) and trust (expectancy) that rewards will follow accomplishment. These can be tempered by reality—the capacity of the organization or the job to provide desired rewards (refer again to your work on **Exercise 1.2**, but this time look at Column 3).

Researchers have found considerable empirical support for this model. In general, the higher the predicted motivation (based on valence, expectancy and instrumentality scores), the greater the effort. Unfortunately, no single model can be used to explain or predict with total accuracy. We are all complex individuals with multiple objectives, varying abilities to predict outcomes, and limited informa-

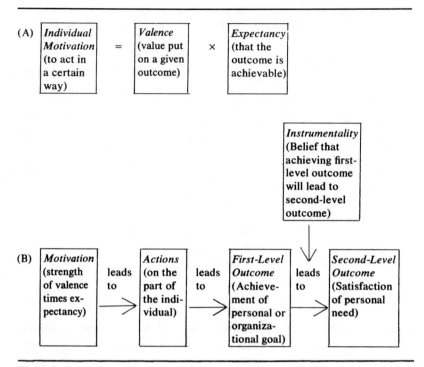

Figure 1   Schematic version of expectancy model (Vroom, 1964).

tion about what is truly possible in a given situation. Lawler suggests that these variations can be accommodated somewhat by expanding the diagram to include different expectations and valences. You may find my rendering of Lawler's schematization helpful in examining your own work-related behavior and that of colleagues (see Figure 2).

Using this model, let's make some educated guesses about Harvey Marcus's thought processes. The amount of effort Harvey puts into seeking support for new projects and setting up a negotiations process is based on his perceptions of his own abilities and capabilities (expectancy 1-2). He further expects (expectancy 2-3) that his performance has a good probability of leading to a grant or contract to set up a complex of innovative community treatment facilities (first-level outcome 3). That performance and the effort that goes into it will be further enhanced by the importance (valence 3) that this outcome has

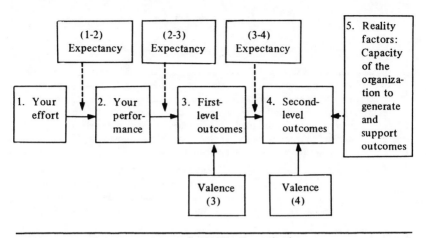

Figure 2   Alternate version of Lawler's (1973) schematization.

for him. In turn, getting the grant or contract may have import (valence 3) to the extent that he expects (expectancy 3-4) that it will lead to a better service, important changes and recognition for his efforts (second-level outcome 4). To the extent that he puts a great deal of value on each of these possible outcomes (valence 4) and believes that they are achievable (expectancy 3-4), his efforts are likely to be considerable.

Over time, Harvey's efforts are likely to continue to be high wherever he puts a lot of store (valence) in the outcome and is reasonably certain of its achievability (expectancy). But this is dependent to a large extent on reality factors that may be outside his control. Other agencies may compete effectively for the same contracts or awards; downturns in the economy or changes in public policy may result in priority shifts; a reshuffling of state-level personnel may require returning to ground one and establishing his (and his agency's) credentials all over again. Thus the costs and likelihood of success may outweigh the potential benefits, especially when equal effort might be invested elsewhere—someplace that might yield a greater likelihood (expectancy) of success.

Moreover, Harvey's circumstances and his own motives may change. Having arrived at a relatively secure and respected position within his agency and in the broader human service community,

Exercise 1.4

Application of the Expectancy Model to Your Practice

1. Using the same schematization we found helpful in analyzing Harvey Marcus's thought processes, analyze your own. Begin by spelling out your desired second-level outcomes. You may find that you've already identified them in **Exercise 1.2**. Then spell out your desired first-level outcomes. How much importance do you place on each? Rate each high, medium or low.

2. Now indicate what you will have to do to get to your first-level outcome (your performance). To what extent do you have the requisite skills, knowledge or other capacities to perform adequately (expectancy 1-2)? Again, give yourself a high, medium or low rating.

3. If you perform well, what is the likelihood (expectancy 2-3) of achieving your first-level objective (high, medium, or low)? What is the likelihood that this achievement will lead to your desired second-level outcome (high, medium or low; expectancy 3-4)? What are some of the reality factors (5) that can support your expectations? Consider agency policies, work climate, availability of resources and any other factors you think may be significant.

4. Based on these considerations, is the effort worth making? What changes in reality factors or in your own capacities are necessary to increase the likelihood of achieving both of the desired (first- and second-level) outcomes?

5. With whom should these thoughts be shared?
    —your supervisor
    —your colleagues at work
    —your spouse or significant other
    —others (specify)_____

6. How might such sharing improve
    —your practice
    —the practices of your supervisors or colleagues
    —your relationship to a significant other
    —your satisfaction on the job
    —your motivation to increase your efforts
    —the ways in which planning and work assignments are made at the agency
    —the ways in which rewards for effort and success are allocated in the agency?

Harvey may be ready to consolidate his gains and protect his investments. With age and experience, he may become more interested in service than in change. This may be expressed by a reduced "hunting urge" and greater commitment to protecting home and property (those programs already established and those clients served by them).

REVIEW AND TENTATIVE CONCLUSIONS

We have explored the contributions of a number of researchers and theorists to our understanding of jobs, job satisfaction and work motivation. And we have completed a number of exercises aimed at increasing our understanding of our own situations. You may have found one or more of the approaches useful and generated a number of insights into your own behavior. I'm going to list some general conclusions I've come to based on my understanding of the concepts discussed. I'll then leave you with room to add your own.

(1) Lower level needs, when unsatisfied, can motivate us to seek changes and improvements, including greater efforts on the job. But lower level needs, once substantially satisfied, no longer act as motivators.

(2) In contrast, higher order needs, when satisfied, lead to greater striving, especially when there are no unmet lower level needs. This is most true of the need to grow and to self-actualize—needs that, once activated, are difficult to turn off. Moreover, higher order needs can be acted on simultaneously. Thus we can work on our social needs (fulfilling expectations of belonging and friendship, esteem and recognition) and our personal needs (being of service, changing things, growing professionally and personally) at the same time.

(3) There is no evidence that being happy at work and feeling satisfied with one's circumstances lead to greater effort or increased motivation (productivity). In fact, there is more evidence to the contrary—that being or feeling productive can be rewarding in its own right or can lead to other rewards.

(4) For some people, job satisfaction is not a means to achieving other ends. It may be an end in itself and should be so considered.

(5) All of us have preferences among the various outcomes that are potentially the result of our efforts. Our expectations that certain actions will lead to desired outcomes will lead to greater efforts on our parts, especially if those outcomes are important to us, and if experience suggests that they are likely.

(6) Clarification of these factors can lead to more effective behavior on our part and on the part of others in the workplace, as well as those outside of work whose respect and esteem we value.

YOUR ADDITIONS

(7)

(8)

(9)

(10)

(11)

(12)

Exercise 1.5

Motivation/Satisfier

Read over the 15 items below. Put an X in each box that applies. Don't take too much time. Just X the items that most strongly reflect your concerns.

If I were looking for a job today, the things I would be most concerned about are:

_____ 1. The extent to which I can be myself on the job.

_____ 2. How well I fit in, whether I will feel accepted or as a stranger.

_____ 3. Opportunities for teamwork and collaborative efforts.

_____ 4. The salary being offered.

_____ 5. Opportunities for advancement, assuming good performance.

_____ 6. The extent to which the work I do will be really meaningful.

_____ 7. Opportunities for growth and development.

_____ 8. The kinds of health and other benefits available to employees.

_____ 9. The relationship I will have with my supervisor.

_____ 10. Whether by taking this job I can be of help to others.

_____ 11. Whether by taking this job I can contribute to the kinds of social change I think important.

_____ 12. How safe the workplace is, and how safe its location.

_____ 13. What others might expect of me.

_____ 14. Whether I will be recognized for my contributions.

_____ 15. The extent to which this is likely to be a stressful place.

(Exercise 1.5 continued next page)

Now circle the number of statements you Xed in the grid below.

A	B	C
4	2	1
5	3	6
8	9	7
12	13	10
15	14	11

If your responses resulted in a preponderance of circles in Column A, you are security-oriented, concerned about income, advancement, benefits and safety. If your responses resulted in a preponderance of circles in Column B, you tend to be social in your orientation, putting emphasis on relationships with others and recognition of your efforts. If your responses resulted in a preponderance of circles in Column C, you tend to be concerned about self-fulfilling accomplishments, doing things that are worthwhile and helpful.

REFERENCES

Alderfer, Clayton P. (1972). *Existence, relatedness and growth: Human needs in organizational settings*. New York: Free Press.

Aronson, Edward, & Carlsmith, J. M. (1962). "Performance expectancy as a determinant of actual performance." *Journal of Abnormal and Social Psychology,* Spring.

D'Arcy, Carl, Syrotuik, John, & Siddique, C. (1984) "Perceived job attributes, job satisfaction and psychological distress: A comparison of working men and women." *Human Relations 37*(8).

Davett, Cynthia. (1983). "Evaluation of the impact of feedback and performance and motivation." *Human Relations, 36*(7).

Farrell, Daniel, & Rusbult, Caryl E. (1981). "Exchange variables as predictors of job satisfaction, job commitment, and turnover: The impact of reward, costs, alternatives, and investments. *Organizational Behavior and Human Performance, 28*(1).

Garland, Howard, & Berwick Smith, Gail. (1981). "Occupational achievement motivation as a function of biological sex, sex-linked personality and occupational stereotypes." *Psychology of Women,* Summer.

Glicken, Virginia. (1980). "Enhancing work for professional social workers." *Administration in Social Work,* Fall.

Herzberg, Fredrick. (1976). *The managerial choice: To be efficient or to be human.* Homewood, IL: Dow-Jones Irwin.

Herzberg, Fredrick, Mauser, Bernard, & Snyderman, Barbara. (1959). *The motivation to work* (2nd ed.). New York: John Wiley.

Kaplan, Abraham (1964). *The conduct of inquiry.* San Francisco: Chandler.

Lawler, Edward E. III. (1973). *Motivation in work organizations.* Monterey, CA: Brooks/Cole.

Lawler, Edward E. III. (1977). "Developing a motivating work climate." *Management Review,* July.

Lawler, Edward E. III, & Porter, Lyman W. (1967). "The effect of performance on job satisfaction." *Industrial Relations,* October.

Maslow, Abraham H. (1954). *Motivation and personality.* New York: Harper & Row.

McClelland, David C. (1961). *The achieving society.* New York: D. Van Nostrand.

Pierce, Jone L. (1983). "Job attitudes and motivation differences between volunteers and employees from comparable organizations." *Journal of Applied Psychology, 28*(4).

Porter, Lyman M., Lawler, Edward E. III, & Hackman, Richard. (1975). *Behavior in organizations.* New York: Mc Graw-Hill.

Quick, Thomas L. (1982). *Understanding people at work.* Englewood Cliffs, NJ: Prentice-Hall.

Richardson, Mary, & West, Peggy. (1982). "Motivational management: Coping with burnout." *Hospital and Community Psychology,* October.

Schoderbeck, P. P., Schoderbeck, C. G., & Plambeck, D. L. (1982). "A comparative analysis of job satisfaction." *Administration in Social Work, 3*(2).

Seybolt, John. (1976). "Work satisfaction as a function of person-environment interaction." *Organizational Behavior and Human Performance,* January.

Tziner, Sharon. (1983). Correspondence between occupational rewards and occupational needs and work satisfaction. *Journal of Occupational Psychology, 57,* Summer.

Voydanoff, Patricia. (1980). Perceived job characteristics and job satisfaction among men and women. *Psychology of Women Quarterly, 5,* Winter.

Vroom, Victor H. (1964). *Work and motivation.* New York: John Wiley.

Chapter 2

RUBBING SHOULDERS AND RUBBING WOUNDS
Gender, Class, Culture, and Identity in the Workplace

Millicent Kapinski was perplexed; disturbed going on devastated might be a better description for how she was feeling. Friday night Yolanda Stephenson and her husband Reggie had been at her home with other members of the staff. It had been a quiet evening, full of good conversation and friendly bantering, marred only by occasional references to budget cuts resulting from shifts in government priority. Millicent had gone out of her way to make Reggie feel comfortable, sensitive to the fact that unlike the others present, he was not a professional and might find some of the discussions outside his interests.

Before leaving, Yolanda had taken Millicent by the hand and expressed how much she enjoyed the evening, how comfortable she had felt, and how much she appreciated the tasteful furnishings and especially the Polish rugs and craftwork which adorned the apartment's walls. "It's so good to be with someone who appreciates her own ethnic heritage, and I wish you would tell me more about the artwork from Chile," referring to the many artifacts Millicent had brought back from her five years in Latin America.

But here it was Tuesday, and Yolanda had barely said a word to her. In fact, when Millicent had invited Yolanda to brown bag it together, she had replied icily: "I don't have to *brown* bag anything, and I don't eat in the office," and turned away. "What's going on?" Millicent wondered.

Ali was wondering the same thing. "Hey," Ali called as Yolanda was going out the door. "If you're eating out today, mind if I join you?" "Not eating today," Yolanda tossed back with a tinge of irritation in her voice. But later at the Sandwiche Shoppe, there was Yolanda sitting in a booth with three other black social workers from the agency. Yolanda had made it a point, Ali was certain, not to see her come in or acknowledge her presence. What *was* going on?

That afternoon, Sam dropped into Yolanda's office for a chat. He had been feeling isolated. His New Americans project was not all that well understood by others at the All-Families Center. Establishing outreach programs for the Southeast Asians—Thais and Vietnamese—who had recently begun to move into the south side, and for Arabs from Iraq, Lebanon and other parts of the Middle East, was new for the agency. Although given considerable latitude in developing the program, this freedom left him feeling insecure, sometimes "as alone and without anchor," he thought, as the people for whom he was trying to develop services. He had decided to seek out Yolanda for advice because he sensed her to be a person committed to the oppressed, and capable of empathy for others.

As he was sketching out some ideas, Yolanda suddenly interrupted, although erupted was more like it: "What's all this garbage about new Americans? You give the Vietnamese a thousand dollars each, and you help the *Ay*-rabs start businesses in Black neighborhoods throwing Blacks out of work. *We're* not new Americans. My family has been slaving away in this country for six generations. Nobody's giving *us* hand-outs. They're keeping us on the dole. Don't talk to me about no new Americans. We got to deal with *old* Americans first. We built this country and we're still on the outside!"

* * * * *

BLACK MAY BE BEAUTIFUL, BUT NOT WHEN YOU GOT TO BE WHITE TO SURVIVE

Clearly, Yolanda's behavior had shocked her white colleagues, but no more than it shocked Yolanda herself. For several weeks now, Yolanda had been lunching on Tuesdays with the other members of what they called the "BiB-Club" (for Black is Beautiful). At first she'd hesitated to join. "Don't want to scare off my white colleagues," Yolanda explained to one of the members. "They might think we're into some kind of plot." Over the years she had carefully built a work identity based on professional competence. She'd been dispassionate in her treatment of clients, both black and white, and had cultivated pleasant and correct relationships with her co-workers at the agency and in other human service organizations. But her professionalism and success on the job were increasingly giving her trouble.

Like many others from racial or cultural minorities, she had been aware of how her integration into agency and professional life had required compromising her cultural self. And like many other Black women, she had consciously chosen to dress and behave in ways that her white colleagues would not find uncomfortable. She'd long ago given up her Afro for a more conservative, straightened hairstyle. Her dress-for-success "uniform" (generally a two-piece dark colored suit and a leather-bound attaché case) was accompanied by a controlled way of walking, and even of laughing and sharing intimacies. But there were no real intimacies. "Being black is *intimate*," Yolanda was aware. Being white, for her, was being *distant*.

That is why she had finally begun to join her Black colleagues in the Tuesday Bib-Club sessions. It was a way of "letting my hair up," she joked to others at the table. Had Ali sat in the next booth, she might have overheard the following snatches of conversation:

"You know, I boogie all the way to work. Got the radio on full force listening to Lionel Richie and any good soul or rock I can find. But I shut it off just before I get into the parking lot. Got to put on the mask. Some of my staff members know I'm into music and like to talk about jazz to me. But it's all that intellectual white "appreciation." Like talking about Fats Waller and Billie Holiday. I mean it's not *today*. Then they talk to me about Alvin Ailey and the Harlem Dance Company. It's condescending, you know? Know what I mean?"

"There's no way I can be *me* at work. It's like my whole chain of black identity is broken when I walk in the door. It's survival, but it's survival without vitality. Sure, we've overcome the barriers of being black and being women, but we're still outsiders."

"It's worse when I go home. My Joe wants me to be cookin' up his chitlins 'n greens and talks about the studs at the garage. I'm taking tranquilizers and he's into booze. It's no life."

"Least you got you a man! My man up and split. Couldn't take it that I was earning more than him and that folks were calling me 'Mrs.' while they was calling him 'Jim.' "

" 'Boy,' you mean."

The feelings expressed in these snatches of conversation are not atypical. Blacks and other minorities in many areas of professional employment find themselves caught between competing identities. As they enter new worlds they face a collision of values, contradictions in life-styles, pulls away from their cultural or ethnic identities. For some, the pressures can become so great as to generate despair that is no less painful than that of the most poverty-stricken ghetto dweller. It can result in a loss of creative vitality, a severing of the Black or other "sinew" which provides the strength to cope with an often hostile or uncaring environment. Similar conclusions can be made about people from other ethnic or cultural backgrounds. Yolanda's responses to Millicent's party, to Ali's invitation to go to lunch together, and to Sam's ideas about immigrant absorption can be understood against this background.

It wasn't until Yolanda had returned home from Millicent's that she realized how different their lives were. She had allowed herself to relax that evening, to enjoy the surroundings, to appreciate a white woman's furnishings and artwork, another person's cultural heritage. And despite her own position at the agency and her own good taste— she had decorated her home on the northwest side of town with the same meticulous care she had lavished on her own grooming—she felt that her own home would never be as natural and without artificiality as Millicent's. The only thing missing, short of an artifact or photograph here or there, was any evidence of her Blackness. "What would I do with African masks?" she wondered, thinking with some jealousy of the tapestries and pottery Millicent had brought back from South America. And yet, despite the absence of artifacts, Yolanda was certain that her white colleagues would have felt uncomfortable in her home.

What had made things worse was Reggie's response to the evening. "Next time we go to your friends' place, we go in *my* car." Reggie drove a Cadillac that he had carefully and lovingly reconditioned. Yolanda, wary of the stereotype, had purchased a small Datsun for going to work and to use on agency business. "I'm not puttin' my black ass in your car," she had retorted. "Want me to act like a nigger?" "You *is* a nigger, a *house* nigger. You ain't got no black ass."

The fight that followed lasted most of the night. The aftermath lasted longer. Through it all, Yolanda was aware that she was undergoing a profound process of reevaluation. She was lucky—lucky that she was a professional social worker and aware of the many reasons for her reactions. But until now these were reasons she had kept carefully tucked away, applying her knowledge to clients but rarely to herself.

The most recent U.S. Census data report that about 300 Black women were divorced for every 1000 marriages—twice the number for whites. Yolanda knew that for Black women with post-B.A. professional training, the figure was 20% higher. She also knew that twice as many Black women were getting professional degrees today as ten years earlier. But for Black men, the percentages had declined by between 10% and 15%. The opportunities that had been opened up for Blacks with the civil rights movement of the 1960s and the Affirmative Action programs of the 1970s had had differential effects for men and women. Yolanda and Reggie were in danger of allowing societal forces to pull them apart.

But Yolanda needed Reggie. She needed the intimacy, the directness of their relationship, the sensuousness in his mannerisms and his movements. Yet she knew that Reggie didn't fit in her predominantly middle-class life-style, a life-style she had never become comfortable with but to which she had clung with the same tenacity with which she had completed school and strived to represent her race and gender at work without ever pushing either. She would break the stereotypes by being good, better than most of her white counterparts at the work she did. But the strains were finally catching up, creating stress that was threatening to unravel everything she had so carefully built, both at home and at work.

By compromising her cultural self, Yolanda had found herself alone, separated from her Black friends no less than from her white colleagues, and from her own husband and his friends. She was certain that the migraines which were beginning to reappear, migraines she had not suffered since college, were symptoms of her isolation. Members of the BiB-Club reported similar psychosomatic symptoms, including menstrual cramps and backaches. Hypertension, diabetes and strokes—common killers of Black women in America—might not be far behind. Tranquilizers, alcohol abuse and cocaine—remedies sought by some of her friends—were not for her.

"Black may be beautiful," she thought, "but not when you got to be white to survive."

* * * * *

OBJECTIFYING OTHERS AT WORK

How white does Yolanda have to be? Harvey Marcus had once objected to her reference to him as white. She had shrugged off his comment without fully understanding the depth from which his remark had come. Yolanda had told him how much she respected his aggressiveness and creativity in seeking new funds and expanding programs for those whom he called "oppressed minorities." "It's easier for you white radical liberals," she had remarked, thinking of how much of an activist Reggie had been when they first met, and how into his car and beer he had become.

"I'm not white," Harvey had responded. "You must be foolin', Harv, you don't look to me like a man of color." "I'm not, but I'm not white either," Harvey had explained with a seriousness that was not normally a part of his demeanor. "I'm Jewish. After the Holocaust, there's no way I could consider myself anything else. You know, it's pretty easy to mistake someone's identity. I was in here one evening in my jeans and a blue workshirt cleaning out some papers, and a new staff member of the children's department asked me to help him move some shelves. He just assumed I was the janitor."[1]

Yolanda had not been ready to deal with Harvey's self-revelation at the time, passing it off with some "dumb remark" she did not remember. But she wondered at it now. And she wondered about Millicent, about Ali and about Sam. Who were they really? Who was she? What were the many pieces that made her into who she was? And why could she not integrate those pieces into a whole personality? Who, besides herself, would she offend in doing so? Who else would she offend if she could not?

A competent professional, Yolanda was aware of the injunction, "Physician, heal thyself." She set out to do so, painful and risky as the process might be. She began by looking at how she perceived others at work, rather than the ways in which she might imagine they perceived her. "I know me," she reasoned. "I don't know them."

In fact, she had painted them, she realized, monochromatically. But Harvey objected to being painted white. Did he also object to her defining him as a "radical liberal," even if the labeling was done in jest? How much fun was there in her remark; how much resentment? She recalled having had difficulty with his name when they first got to know each other. "This is Harvey Shapiro," she had once introduced him to a friend. But Harvey's last name was Marcus. Why the confusion in names? Was she also stereotyping him? Name confusion, she realized, often occurs when we are objectifying others, defining them in stereotypic ways, or treating them as part of a "class" in an effort to assign to them certain categories of thought and behavior. As a Black and a woman, she had been the victim of similar slips of the tongue more than once.

Although she had met Millicent long after the older woman had left the Church, Yolanda still thought of her as "the nun," visualizing her in a black habit. Perhaps that was why she had been so shocked to find Millicent's home so warm, and so tastefully and ethnically furnished. Somehow her image of a nun had been different. She had expected a more stark environment.

And what about Sam? His middle name, Faoud, added to his round shape and Mediterranean complexion, brought to mind images of King Farouk, the deposed monarch of Egypt she had first learned about in high school. Sometimes she even thought of him as a monarch, smiling to herself at the designation, and resenting the fact that he was becoming "king" of all those new immigrants. Objectification again? For sure. In truth, Sam had none of the mannerisms associated with the real Farouk. He was a decent, hard-working man, as committed, perhaps more so, to his constituents as she was to her people. No wonder she felt resentment. It wasn't Sam she was resenting as much herself and the centuries of isolation, racism and persecution her own people had suffered. Why take it out on Sam and his new Americans?

Her feelings about Ali were more complex, more difficult to come to terms with. "Why was I so damned irritated when she invited me to lunch? It wasn't just that I was sneaking off to a meeting of the Bib-Club; it was something more. By the grace of God, and my own hard work," Yolanda realized, "I could have been in Ali's job, nothing more than a receptionist. '*Nothing more* than a receptionist!' " Had she absorbed society's sexist and racist definitions? Was she saying that Blacks should be receptionists and had no right to be administrators in an agency? Was she resenting the respect Ali received for the way she did her work, even though she had no professional qualifications? Was she downgrading Ali's contributions to the agency because of a class bias? She would have to work on this one, she realized. It's no easy thing to confront your own bias and your own pain!

Perhaps it's time now to confront some of *your* pain—as a man or woman, member of a racial or ethnic minority, native born or foreign born, new or experienced staff member, heterosexual or gay, young in age or older.

* * * * *

WOMEN'S WORK

Perhaps it is time to find out a bit more about Ali and Millicent. If Ali were to be asked, she would tell everyone she loves her job. "I don't know if I was made for this kind of work or if the job was made for me," she told her mother a few weeks after beginning work at the agency. That was eight years ago.

Ali likes to manage. She always has. As the eldest of five siblings, she had helped her mother with chores around the house, caring for the younger children. After her mother had taken ill—Ali was 11 at the time—she took over the household until her mother regained her strength and was able to return home. No one spoke much about the hospital[2] where Mrs. Schultz had been confined for two years, but Ali knew it had something to do with her mother's depression. Ali's mother had never been a strong person. Even when she returned home, she seemed content, even relieved that Ali was able to take such good care of her three school-aged brothers and her baby sister.

Ali and her father, a foreman at the Stroh's brewery, had grown closer after her mother had been hospitalized, but it had seemed to Ali that as she grew older, that closeness was built on her father's dependence—a dependence that did not disappear when her mother returned. "I'm not cut out for housework and bringing up kids," her father had once told her. "Thank God I have you." Ali liked being needed.

Although she did not do particularly well at school—there was never enough time to do school-related homework with so much "real" homework to do—her teachers liked Ali and gave her good marks on her report cards, more perhaps for her pleasant manner than her intellectual contributions. But Ali's school work was always neat and turned in on time. "Competent" and "a contributor" were adjectives nearly always handwritten on the "work habits" and "citizen-

Exercise 2.1

Confronting the Pain

Think back on instances in which you were treated as a member of a class with the expectation that you would think or behave in some stereotypic manner—a manner that was more than painful.

1. How did you feel about it?

2. How did you respond?

3. What was the response to your response?

4. How should you have responded?

Now that you've examined how others look at you and your responses, take a look at how you view them.

ship" columns. The only negative comment she remembered was from her fifth grade teacher, who wrote "bites her nails too much." This had embarrassed Ali.

Ali was a good citizen. She had to be. It was expected of her. And if she was not competent, who would be? Now with her youngest sister still in high school, Ali continued to live at home, getting up early to fix breakfast for her father, who had to be at the plant by 7:00 a.m., and

Exercise 2.2

Objectification Assessment

Look over your assessments of Yolanda and the others in **Exercise 1.1** of the first chapter. Because information on each of the six staff members was so brief, you were forced to make some assumptions about each. You may not know much more at this point about the other three names you yourself added.

1. Begin by checking whether your assessment was in some way based on objectification by gender, race/ethnicity or class.

2. Jot down some of your thoughts about why you responded as you did. Follow as thoroughly honest a process as Yolanda did. It won't be easy.

OBJECTIFIED BY:

	Gender	Race/ Ethnicity	Class	Your Thoughts
Yolanda				
Sam				
Ali				
Millicent				
Carl				
Harvey				
1.				
2.				
3.				

Martha, who had a 7:15 a.m. Driver's Ed class. This gave her plenty of time to get to the office early, turn on the lights, plug in the coffee, and put the day's schedule in order.

When Yolanda had run out in a huff and then ignored her at the Sandwiche Shoppe, Ali had been thrown into a near panic. She sat at a table alone, unable to touch her food. It felt almost like the day they had taken her mother to the hospital. Ali bought a pack of cigarettes, the first she had opened in three months. Back at work, Ali had pushed any disquieting and depressing thoughts to the back of her mind and reasserted her outward pleasantness. But something seemed empty inside. It felt only a slight bit better at the end of the day when Yolanda stopped by to say she was sorry about being so gruff, that she'd had something on her mind and needed to talk it over with some friends. "But I'm your friend, too," Ali thought, resentful of Yolanda's preference for being with other Black women.

For Yolanda, the apology was not without effort. "She seems so comfortable in her work, like a busy housewife. She's all things I can't seem to be. All the things I've been running away from. Maybe that's what irritates me so," she thought as she inched out of the driveway and reached absentmindedly for the car radio.

* * * * *

Millicent Kapinski was the seventh of eight children and the only girl. Not much had been expected of her as she grew up. A quiet child, the only one in the family without a Polish or Catholic name, Millicent never felt that she quite fit in the family. Given to daydreaming and drawing pictures in her schoolbooks, Mili (she never liked the nickname either) did not have very many friends. She cried bitterly when Mary, her best friend, moved out of the neighborhood.

The first two years of high school were a nightmare for Millicent. She thanked God that her parents had seen fit to send her to parochial school. But even there, the talk among her girlfriends was always about boys and sex. She just did not want to think about boys that way and was equally disgusted by her brothers' talk at home and the innuendos and often overt sexual approaches by John and Stash. She remembered with shame how they had once made her "pee" standing up. She had never confessed this to a priest, and the shame of it was something she could not rid herself of. Priests were men, like her brothers. How could they be trusted?

Her first sense of being someone came when one of the sisters at school approached her to ask that she tutor younger children for their catechism. She loved tutoring younger children and soon volunteered to help out in the Sunday morning day care center in her parish. Later she joined the Latin and Spanish clubs at school, and to her surprise was elected president of the latter. Here, for the first time, she found herself expressing ideas and taking responsibility for special projects. And she liked the feel of it.

No one was surprised when Millicent decided to join Sacred Heart and become a teacher. For Millicent, it had seemed the natural thing to do. She was good with children, cared about them and wanted to reach out to others who, like herself, felt isolated and alone as they were growing up.

Sister Peter Claver, as she was now known, was a fine teacher, creative and caring, well liked by parents, children and colleagues. Her Mother Superior, a warm and supportive woman, saw in the young nun an imaginative educator. She would probably still be teaching today if it had not been for the civil rights movement of the late 1960s and early 1970s. Increasing numbers of Black children were enrolling in the school as white Catholics moved out of the neighborhood and the church reached out to those less fortunate. She sensed in herself a prejudice about many of the children and had a difficult time understanding their English. "Am I being racist in the way I feel about them?" she wondered.

Sister Peter did a lot of reading about the Black community. She read *Malcolm X Speaks,* Frantz Fanon and others who spoke with a radical and angry voice. And then she found her way to Paolo Friere's *Pedagogy of the Oppressed,* and other writings by liberationalist theologians. She was not alone in her discovery of new and challenging ideologies. There were others in her order, as well as Jesuits at the nearby seminary, who were exploring the same ideas. It was not long before she found herself in the company of Catholic men and women, some of whom had "gone over the wall," who were as questioning of both the church and their own beliefs as she was. Finding herself increasingly in conflict with Church policy over birth control and abortion, she finally came to the conclusion that there were too many pregnant teenagers, "too much despair, delinquency and substance abuse" around her that others refused to see. If her way was blocked within the Church, she would find a way of dealing with these issues outside it.

After 20 years of teaching, Millicent quietly resigned from her job and her order, took off her habit and returned to the university where she earned a master's degree in adult and continuing education. "That first semester I could hardly concentrate on my studies. I didn't know who I was. I was grieving, grieving for a lost identity and I had to find a new one. Crazy, isn't it? Here I was, 42 years old and I didn't know who I was. Life as I had experienced it had gone sour. Doing my rosaries was no solace." The company and support of other former clerics (she shared a house near the campus with two former nuns and two ex-priests) gave her strength to pass through months of crisis. "I came out of it all the stronger, my own woman for the first time."

On completing her M.A., Millicent and another former nun traveled to South America, where they worked at first in small villages in Argentina. In the beginning she felt helpless, as helpless as the Indian villagers with whom she worked. "Are they really capable of change?" she asked herself. The more she worked with the poor, the more she realized that the problem was not in them but in herself. She began to probe her own childhood, her biases, her own racist feelings. All her readings and all her teaching skill, she came to understand, were of no use unless she could understand her own responses to the situation in which she found herself. If these self-confrontations were so difficult for her, she realized, how much more difficult must they be for the villagers? Yet simple people as they were, she found them open to change and growth. She must grow with them.

It was the only way she could deal with her own malignancy—the same class and ethnic biases that led to the oppression (and acceptance of oppression) of those she had set out to help. When the political climate made further educational and community development efforts unsafe, she went first to Chile and then decided to return home. By that time she had developed a critical consciousness— "conscienizacion," as it was called in Latin America. And she had learned to use *conscienizacion* as a training tool for helping others understand themselves in their situations. It was as much a political as an educational process.

Teachers like herself, in interaction with local people acting collectively, could make a difference. The difference emerged from relationships that led people to "name the world"—that is, to reperceive their personal and social realities, recognizing that neither were fixed, that through critical awareness and action one could synthesize one's values and take responsibility for both self- and communal development. The unity she had once sought in the Trinity she now found in a dialectic of thought and action that led to a renewed commitment to becoming.

Now, six years later, Millicent had integrated both her philosophy and her skills and applied them to the family education programs conducted under the agency's auspices. Her current situation was not without strain, but Millicent was not a flaming militant. She was too old for that. "It might have been different if I had matured earlier," she thought. The best thing a "retread" can do is provide a safe and comfortable ride. And that is how she saw herself—as a support to both clients and staff in their efforts to become and to arrive at destinations of their own choosing.

Others on the staff sought Millicent out on their off hours. She accepted them with whatever they brought—not seeking their confessions but careful not to set up barriers to communication or to engender guilt and fearful emotions. She still recalled her early experience in the confessional booth. "I listen and I probe a bit, trying to get others to reach a little beyond themselves. Maybe I'm a little too pushy sometimes. Guess that's why I've become everyone's Polish mother, with a bit of Mother Superior thrown in."

That is also why she did not take offense at Yolanda's "brown bag" remark. "She's feeling some pain," Millicent thought. "Women understand pain, and that's a good start for any dialogue."

UNDERSTANDING PAIN

Like Yolanda, Ali and Millicent, none of us are free of gender, racial, and class biases. But to recognize those biases, especially if we ourselves have been victimized by them, takes considerable courage. It entails great risk, both to the defenses we have set up and to the definitions of ourselves we have created to support a positive self-image. And if we strip either defenses or definitions away, what will be left?

Millicent learned, albeit late in life, that in order to help others confront the conditions of racism and classism, she had first to confront those feelings in herself. Unless she did, there was no way she could ask her childhood confessional priest, or the Indian villagers with whom she worked, for forgiveness. Asking for such forgiveness required ascribing to them a goodness she did not feel in herself. But asking others to forgive us assumes that they possess qualities that we do not. And since they are likely to be equally crippled by bias and ignorance, we are bound to be disappointed in them as we are in ourselves. Objectifying others by ascribing superior values or capacities to them can be as crippling as ascribing negative values to them. Both are nonstarters. Guilt and self-doubt are feelings, and we are not, Millicent had come to understand, to be blamed for our feelings. Her South American experience had taught her that feelings are to be dealt with for the sake or our own liberation. We are none of us ever quite free of ourselves and our situations.

Yolanda was taking the first steps toward such recognition in confronting her feelings about her husband, her co-workers, and herself. But what of Ali? She seems to have carved out a niche for herself, a comfortable one. If one asked her, she would shrug off with a smile any suggestion that she too suffered from oppression. Yolanda's assessment would seem to confirm Ali's own. Perhaps it is not Ali's apparent satisfaction in her situation that nags at Yolanda so, but rather the budding recognition that beneath Ali's pleasantness and competence is a person just as oppressed by the need to respond to the expectations and praises of others as Yolanda often feels because of her black skin and the prejudices of a society that has not rid itself of racism and sexism.

Each of the staff members in the agency, as is the case for each of its clients, suffers some pain. We have only touched on Yolanda's, Ali's, and Millicent's, and we have barely scratched the surface of Sam's, Harvey's, and Carl's. It is not likely that these agency workers will resolve the conflicts and contradictions in their lives that we generally refer to in shorthand as "hang-ups." But Millicent and Yolanda have taken major steps to confront theirs.

For Millicent, this required taking on a new identity and redefining her situation in political terms. For Yolanda, the process of reevaluation is taking a psychological and sociological turn, in keeping with the knowledge and skills she has developed as a social worker. For Ali, an awakening, if it is to occur, may stem from the feelings of anxiety she experienced from Yolanda's apparent rejection. For all three, childhood experiences and the process of growing up and entering the world of work were central factors. For Yolanda, being Black in America is at the core of her identity. It is perceived by her as the major factor in understanding her behavior and responses to others.

Exercise 2.3

Confronting Your Own Pain

Jot down some incidents in which relationships with colleagues, supervisors, subordinates or clients at work touched at the core of your identity—incidents that caused real pain.

1.

2.

3.

Now jot down situations in which something you said or did touched an identity nerve in someone else. Was it a gender nerve, class nerve, race or ethnic identity nerve?

1.

2.

3.

HELP FROM THE BEHAVIORAL SCIENCES

Each of us has a psychosocial-biological developmental history and a racial-gender-cultural history which help shape our behavior. We need not be nonassertive captives of our pasts. To the contrary, these histories give meaning to the present and make it possible to shape the future responsibly.

I will briefly recap the contributions of two men to our understanding of personal development: Freud and Erikson. You are probably already acquainted with their concepts. In fact, I have selected them because of their familiarity. I recognize that the ideas that each man propounded generated some controversy, and that more recent contributions to the scientific literature have both supported and challenged what each of these "stage theorists" has to teach us. Sigmund Freud, whose theories, according to Jerome Bruner, might better be characterized as "metaphor," or "drama," was the first in modern times to stress that impulses below the level of awareness have an impact on our feelings and behavior. According to Freud, the struggle between instinctive drives (libido) and societal prohibitions is what gives rise to both personality and behavior. Those impulses that are considered antisocial and for which we are punished or threatened are turned inward only to find new expression as hang-ups, neuroses, dreams, slips of the tongue, art and literature, religion and ideology, myth and other cultural and personal expressions.

Freud postulated five libidinal or psychosocial stages through which all human beings pass. Should we be unsuccessful in resolving conflicts at any of these stages, the resulting frustration may lead to inappropriate and even bizarre behavior. For some, the pleasures associated with each stage may result in fixation and a subconscious refusal to move on to the next stage of development. For example, Freud thought that the source of conflict in the *oral* stage (birth to 18 months) is the cessation of breast feeding or a satisfactory substitute. Fixation at this stage may lead to insatiable demands for mothering (which may be sublimated into its opposite, the need to mother others), verbal abuse, excessive oral behaviors like compulsive eating and nail biting, smoking, and alcoholism.

Children passing through the *anal* stage (18 to 36 months) face potential conflict at the point of toilet training, sometimes finding outlets in such later behaviors as superconformity and preoccupation with rules, compulsive neatness, or in defiance of authority and eruptions of hostility. The *phallic* stage (3 to 7 years) can lead to the Oedipal complex in boys and the Electra complex in girls. In adult life these can be expressed as fear of sexual relationships, frigidity or impotence, homosexuality or difficulty in handling competitive relationships.

Although he considered them of lesser importance in shaping adult personality, Freud also postulated two other stages. The *latency* period is associated with the elementary school years in which boys learn to behave like boys and girls like girls. Sexual reawakening at puberty launches a *genital* period in which equilibriums established earlier are upset. Social and political commitments, romantic attachments to people and causes are born here and may significantly influence occupational choice and personal identity.

Freud and his followers described a number of ego defenses that people use to protect themselves from the pain associated with the anxiety and emotional conflict arising from incomplete or unsuccessful coping in earlier stages:

(1) *repression* (driving a threatening thought or impulse from conscious awareness in an effort to avoid anxiety and guilt);

(2) *displacement* (taking out one's frustration or pent-up hostility on someone "safe," usually someone weaker who cannot or will not strike back—instead of at those directly responsible for our discomfort—a process associated with scapegoating);

(3) *projection* (in which persons attribute their own feelings of rage or prejudice to others because the otherwise resultant feelings of guilt and self-blame might be too difficult to bear);

(4) *denial* (refusal to acknowledge an unpleasant reality);

(5) *sublimation* (in which unacceptable behaviors are repressed only to reemerge in a more socially acceptable form, as for example when rage is turned to social activism);

(6) *regression* (in effect, returning to an earlier and less pressured stage when under heavy strain or stress);

(7) *reaction-formation* (behaving in ways that are directly opposite to one's inclinations because those inclinations are for some reason unacceptable to the actor); and

(8) *rationalization* (by which people find convincing reasons for acting in ways they might otherwise find unacceptable).

If you have had analytic training or are working in an agency that employs analytically oriented therapies, these terms will be familiar to you. On the one hand, you will know enough to realize that quick diagnoses can be harmful, leading to the same process of objectification that we discussed with regard to race, class, ethnicity, and gender. Besides, what good would it do to define Ali's personality as oral, Yolanda's as anal, or Millicent's as compounded by an Electra complex? On the other hand, awareness of ego defenses can be helpful.

Clearly, Millicent understood Yolanda's anger as *displacement*. Will she be equally aware of the extent to which her professional choices have been a *sublimation* of other less (to her) acceptable behaviors? Yolanda, as she pursues her own efforts to understand the reactions she has to other staff members, will recognize that her desire not to offend whites through unacceptable dress and mannerisms is at least partially related to projective mechanisms, an expression of her own racial and cultural biases. On the surface of things, Ali seems to have it pretty well together. But the anxiety, almost a feeling of panic, she experienced following Yolanda's rejection—her nervous nail biting and return to smoking—suggest that she is a prisoner of a variety of repressions.

Helpful as these constructs are in understanding behavior, you may find Erikson's expanded stages of development even more useful. Erik Erikson, a trained psychoanalyst, possessed a deep sense of history and an appreciation for the methods and concepts derived from anthropology. Much of his research focused on the development of personality and identity. Unlike Freud, he put considerable emphasis on the later stages of development.

According to Erikson, healthy psychosocial development occurs only with the successful resolution of crises at each of eight stages. These stages are labeled (1) infancy; (2) early childhood; (3) fourth to sixth year; (4) sixth year to onset of puberty; (5) adolescence; (6) young adulthood; (7) adulthood; and (8) old age. Although Erikson's work has also been criticized for being too global (especially with regard to the latter two stages, which might be subdivided into more segments that reflect additional crises), we can learn a great deal from it. Keep in mind that a number of researchers have accepted the eight stages described by Erikson but, unlike him, have concluded that personality and identity continue to develop in adulthood as people cope with new challenges and situations.

Infancy (birth to one year) is that stage in which a person learns trust or mistrust. Those who experience consistent and genuine affection, cuddling and responsive care come to view the world as safe and dependable. In contrast, those whose infancy is unpredictable, chaotic or characterized by rejection are likely to perceive the world with fear and suspicion. In early childhood (second and third years), the child explores and develops motor skills. Those who are allowed freedom without overprotection are likely to mature into autonomous individuals, freed of the shame and fear that might otherwise accompany attempting new tasks without sufficient competence or skill.

The theme of freedom is again central to the fourth and fifth years. Those overly confined or restricted are not likely to assume initiative in later life. To the contrary, they are more likely to experience the impulse to be different and creative with a sense of guilt and foreboding. As the child enters and progresses through elementary school, he or she develops either a sense of industry, of mastery over self and environment, or of inferiority and the inability to compete successfully. It is often at this stage that differences in expectations for boys and girls may shape their self-concepts. In some communities, the expectations may be different for whites or Blacks, Hispanics or Anglos, or for children from middle-class or working-class families. Children may be tracked into different careers and may perceive their life chances according to how they are perceived by others.

Adolescence is that stage when young people try on different identities, shedding uncomfortable ones for others they think might fit better. But the turbulence in this period can also result in role confusion, an inability to develop a centered, positive identity. This is also a period when identity can be shaped by taking on a calling, an ideology, a commitment to people by means of a faith or ideology. The capacity to develop intimacy, to identify with others, to share, care and empathize may occur in young adulthood. The fear of rejection, however, may generate shallow relationships, withdrawal and isolation.

Adults, according to Erikson, if they have dealt successfully with earlier challenges, can reach out beyond their immediate concerns to embrace the well-being of their children and the welfare of others— the society, a particular subgroup or even future generations. He calls this *generativity*. In contrast, some adults become self-centered, concerned only with their own physical well-being and the accumulation of possessions. These Erikson describes as boxed into a process of stagnation. All adults, according to him, strive for some unity, for the integration of their many selves and many experiences. But some see no unity and feel no satisfaction for what they are or for what they have accomplished. Thus, as they approach old age, some may become overwhelmed by a sense of despair, a feeling that there is just insufficient time left to right the many wrongs, to take another path or to try out an alternative road to integrity.

Bernice Neugarten, a sociologist who has concentrated much of her research on the elderly, concludes that age alone is not a decisive factor in personality development—that given the right environment and encouragement, people at any age can grow in their capacities to trust, become more autonomous, assume guilt-free initiative, achieve, take on new roles and assume more positive identities, establish intimacy, assume responsibility for others, and arrive at a sense of wholeness and integrity.

To what extent does your workplace provide the context for such development? To what extent are the agency's environment, its procedures and rules more likely to generate distrust, doubt, guilt, inferiority, role-confusion, isolation, stagnation and even despair? What accounts for your answers: the personalities involved, the agency's rules and procedures, or the expectations imposed on it by forces outside the agency (e.g., accountability mechanisms, funder's requirements, relationships to other agencies, expectations of clients)?

There are two other major schools of psychology, both of which take exception to the developmental psychologists represented by Freud and Erikson. Each may contribute some additional insights into the behavior of the staff member we have been observing and that of individuals in your own workplace. One school is generally associated with the label of "behaviorism" and the other with "humanistic" psychology.

The behaviorist paradigm or model of reality is considerably different from the developmental approach. In most ways, the two models are irreconcilable. Yet we can learn much from each. Behaviorists begin with the assumption that scientists must restrict themselves to observations of behavior. According to them, assumptions about hidden meanings or inferences about cause made from the examination of symptoms is art, not science. Although most behaviorists no longer believe, as did John Watson, a pioneer in American psychology, that all behavior is learned and that none of it is the result of heredity or biology, the influences and stimuli of the environment continue to be of paramount importance in their analysis.

As early behavioral experimentation by B. F. Skinner and others has demonstrated, people (and animals) learn both to generalize and to discriminate in response to stimuli. *Stimulus generalization* refers to the learned ability to match new sensory inputs (sights, sounds, tastes, smells, or touches) with previously absorbed and similar information. The greater the perceived resemblance between the original stimulus and the new situation, the greater the likelihood of a similar (and strong) response. This makes it possible to assimilate earlier experiences, to learn from them, and to apply our learning to new situations. For example, Yolanda's rush out of the agency was perceived by Ali as a form of personal rejection (perhaps related to the sudden hospitalization of Ali's mother). Yolanda's hypersensitivity to hints of racism is a similar example of stimulus generalization.

In contrast, *stimulus discrimination* refers to the ability to discriminate between relevant information and irrelevant information by responding to the former and ignoring the latter. Thus Millicent was able to discriminate between Yolanda's apparent rage and the causes of that rage, which had little to do with Millicent herself. In fact, her work in Latin America and her embracing of *conscienizacion* gave her a strategic tool for helping others reexamine how they respond to and understand the situations in which they find themselves. But Yolanda was trapped in confusion between generalization and discrimination in her responses to the stimuli of the evening at Millicent's. Inappropriate (mistaken) stimulus generalization leads to objectivation, while inappropriate stimulus discrimination can lead to missing important cues.

Appropriate behavioral responses can be reinforced positively, negatively or reciprocally. *Positive reinforcers,* when applied following a behavior, tend to be rewarding. If we want a particular reward and believe that it will be forthcoming—say, pleasant behavior on the part of colleagues or an increase of responsibility on the job (recall Vroom's and Porter's work on expectancy theory discussed in Chapter 1)—we are likely to act (put in the effort) in such a way as to gain the reward. By contrast, *negative reinforcers* may include the removal of a reward or the addition of a penalty or threat of punishment. Finally, *reciprocal reinforcers* are characteristic of much social interaction. Thus Ali's ready smile and her arrangement of the office early in the morning (including the preparation of coffee) lead others to respond to her pleasantly and with some affection. Their responses, in turn, reinforce Ali's desire to please and strengthen her expectation that she will be appreciated (rewarded) for her actions.

You may find these conceptions helpful or limiting. There is still another approach.

Humanistic psychology has sometimes been called a "third force." It is a reaction to the limitations of the traditions of behaviorism and psychoanalysis. Motivation psychologists such as Maslow and others, discussed earlier, maintain that people are different from other organisms in that they actively intervene in the course of events and shape the environments in which they live and work. Their concern is with optimizing the human potential for self-direction and self-actualization.

Carl Rogers, a leading figure in the "human potentials" movement, draws his notion of an environmental "field" from earlier work by Kurt Lewin. Boiling it all down into a nutshell, Rogers suggests the following: Short of pathological behavior, people share a basic desire to maintain and enhance themselves. Their behavior is essentially goal-directed, consisting of efforts to satisfy needs as they are experienced. Experience occurs in a social and material field—the environment. The way in which that environment is perceived is different for each person and constitutes his or her reality. Such perceptions are accompanied by affect, emotions which support (facilitate) or detract from goal-directed behavior. So far, we have some additional support for what we already know about Ali, Millicent, and Yolanda. Clearly, the experience of becoming the substitute mother for one's younger siblings, or of being the only girl in a large family where girls were not much cared about, or growing up Black in a society where occupational success for a Black woman was perceived to be more the exception than the norm, had its effects on the three women as they were growing up. But what of the forces that might lead to growth and change, in contrast with rigidifying their current perceptions and behaviors?

Here, Rogers may be of some further help. He suggests that experiences that are inconsistent with our understanding of ourselves and of the organization of the self may be perceived as a threat. The greater the threat and the more of these perceptions there are, the more likely we are to organize our lives and ourselves so as to hold rigidly to what we are (in contrast to what we can become). The principle is one of self-defense. But removal of objective threats or changes in perception so that we no longer feel a threat to self-structure frees us to examine inconsistent experiences, assimilate these experiences and, in so doing, revise or expand ourselves. Thus human potential is relatively unlimited, and freedom comes with self-actualization.

We have already noted that Millicent and Yolanda are well into this process. Are there conditions in the work environment at the agency that contribute to such a reconstruction of self and reality? We may not have enough information on the agency to make such judgments yet. But what about *your* agency, the setting in which *you* work?

Before moving on, let's take a few moments to discuss still another perspective, one that has to a large extent shaped Millicent's awareness and that may help us to comprehend the French term *travail*. I am referring to the Marxian analysis of work and the forces that shape human behavior. The key concept in Marx's critique of civilization is that of alienation and estrangement. The division of labor in modern life, Marx argued, has led to man's becoming a cog in a wheel. Work, rather than being integrating, has led to fragmentation. Only parts of the person are valued at work; only parts of the person are treated

Exercise 2.4

Using Psychological Theories

Take a moment or two to reflect on what you know about behavior. We have briefly reviewed the major contributions of

—Sigmund Freud and Erik Erikson (psychoanalytic stage theorists)
—John Watson and B. F. Skinner (behaviorists)
—Abraham Maslow and Carl Rogers (humanistic psychologists) and members of the human potentials movement

1. Which of these approaches do you find most useful; least useful? Why?

2. Now take the approach you find most compatible with your own world view (i.e., the one you find most useful) and apply it to a more comprehensive analysis of one of the staff members discussed in this chapter. What else do you need to know? What would you do with this information?

3. Finally, apply the same approach to examining yourself, your response to work-related stimuli and your relations to others on the job. What have you learned? What can you do with what you've learned?

when he or she becomes a patient, client, student, member, voter, and so on.

Through a process Marx called "thingification" *(Verdinglichung),* we have become commodities to be shaped and processed and used or sold by the very institutions we have created. In effect, these institutions repress the very life which brought them into being. The development of critical consciousness, *concienizacion,* is the first step in movement from alienation to a sense of belonging and commitment. Marx's idea of a classless society is not so different from Millicent's search for unity, wholeness, and integration.

For the individual, alienation can be reduced by taking on responsibility, by assuming ownership for one's actions. For the organization or for society, alienation can be reduced by a process of shared decision making, collective action and responsibility. To what extent do these concepts help you to better understand Yolanda's estrangement? Harvey's? Carl's?

GENDER-STEREOTYPING AT WORK:
THE PINK-COLLAR SYNDROME

When it comes to gender studies, anthropologists and sociologists have tended to be as concerned with the differences (in contrast with the similarities) between men and women as have the psychologists. All three groups of social scientists are, in their own ways, embroiled in the arguments on the relative weight of hereditary versus environmental causes of gender-differential behavior. Sex-role stereotypes are almost as pervasive in the scientific literature as they are in other cultural expressions. This in itself is evidence of the impact of culture on gender-related roles and on how each of us deals with the expectations of others as we attempt to fulfill our expectations for ourselves.

We are all aware of the media-supported stereotypes of women as mothering and caring, child-focused, expert at reconciling conflict, concerned with attracting men and often using their sex to do so, capricious and emotional, supportive of their men on the one hand, and subtly outsmarting them on the other, scheming and succoring at the same time—stereotypes as contradictory and old as those associated with Eve. Stereotypes perform a number of interesting functions, regardless of whether they are contradictory or complementary and consistent.

First, they reduce the complexity of social reality into shortcuts to understanding, or at least explaining. Thus behaviors that are both assertive or submissive, clever or childlike, are likely to be found "typical of women." But when they are defined as atypical, the woman in question may be found wanting in femininity or aberrant in her behavior. Stereotypes also enable us to respond to behavioral cues in standard ways (generalization in contrast with differentiation). Standardized responses, while limiting, are often comfortable. The comfort found in sex-stereotyping is as important to women as it is to men. It provides a woman with a sort of touched-up photograph, a treated mirror that enables her to see herself as others (both men and women) do. This looking-glass self becomes the model with which to conform, against which to judge one's own behavior and that of others. Deviation from this image of what one is or ought to be is fraught with danger. It can lead to social ostracism, condemnation, a loss of bearing when one steps "out of place." It can also lead to self-assessment as wicked or inferior, and to feelings of guilt that are associated with the rivalry between women and men.

What has only recently come to be realized is that the new rivalry with men, associated with women's emancipation, or "liberation" if you will, tends to be fought out in two arenas. The first is the general work arena in which women compete with men in occupations that have traditionally been closed to women: business and finance, politics, engineering, and so on. Here women and men have pushed for equal opportunity, equal pay, and other rewards.

The second arena is to be found in specialized occupations in which it has been assumed that women, because of their distinctive qualities, have a special contribution to make. I don't mean secretarial or receptionist work like Ali's. Arguments that women are better suited than men for such jobs can easily be disposed of despite the fact (or perhaps because of it) that they articulate with the biases that relegate women to supportive or secondary positions at work as well as at home.

I am referring instead to the preponderance of women in what have come to be known as the "pink-collar" occupations; nursing, teaching, social work and other human services. Thus even occupations have been dichotomized according to presumed male and female characteristics. The impact that this can have on both career choice and job satisfaction, and on one's personal life, can be illustrated by some of Yolanda's earlier experiences in school and at work.

* * * * *

As an undergraduate, Yolanda had considered majoring either in communications or business—careers, she reasoned, that would pull her forever out of poverty and permit her to put many of her skills to good use. She was discouraged, however, by the anticipated pressures of having to prove herself in work settings where neither women nor Blacks had made any major headway. Volunteer work as a tutor in her sophomore year had given her so much personal satisfaction that she decided social work was both more accessible and more likely to be rewarding—perhaps not in dollars earned, but in terms of acceptance both within the profession itself and within her own family. Her parents would understand social work, and so would her brothers and her friends. But Yolanda still had other dreams.

The first job she took on completing her MSW was as counselor in a GM plant. "If I make it there," she confided to a friend, "maybe I can move into other areas of management." It was at the plant that she had met Reggie, a line foreman whose "style" she felt comfortable with. Yolanda worked hard; she had to. "I felt that if I was successful, I would do something not only for myself, but for women and Blacks too. It was a real motivator.

"I did my work and I did it well, got promoted twice. Then one day I realized the secure structure I'd constructed for myself wasn't built out of bricks at all. It was a flimsy house made of cards and it all came tumbling down." Yolanda had been asked to prepare a proposal for creating an employee assistance program. A concept paper had to be ready in one week. It was, competently and professionally prepared. But it was turned down on review by executives higher up. That in itself did not upset Yolanda.

"What the hell, you can't win on every score. But it's the way my boss handled it that really got to me. 'Sorry, kid, don't sweat it. I guess it was too much pressure to put on a woman.' The bastard really had me in a bind. Here he was trying to be nice, showing me he 'respected' women, but all the time assuming that we couldn't deal with pressures. What did he think, that a man could have done better?"

When Yolanda did well, she had come to realize, she was considered the exception—both as a woman and as a Black. But when she did not succeed, her failures were branded as "collective." Small comfort!

It was about this time that her relationship with Reggie was also coming under some strain. "He just couldn't hack the fact that I was in management, talking to the higher-ups. The guys on the line would razz him about being married to one of the bosses. His being a line foreman didn't make any difference. He still was coming to work in his blues while I wore a black suit and carried an attaché case. 'You don't belong there,' he told me when I told him about the 'pressure on women' remark. He was right.

"That's when I decided to look for a job in a social work agency where I really did belong."

* * * * *

Yolanda's experiences are not atypical. How has sex-stereotyping affected you at work? How did it affect the kind of work you decided to undertake? How would you have reacted to the pressures Yolanda was under? How have you contributed to sex-stereotyping in your agency?

REVIEW AND TENTATIVE CONCLUSIONS

Clearly, rubbing shoulders with others whose histories, psychological reactions, and racial-gender-ethnic-class identities are different from ours can open up scars that we thought long healed. Rubbing shoulders at work can rub old wounds sore.

What conclusions can we draw from all this? I'll list a few. You should then review the chapter and your own work experiences and add others.

(1) Men and women, blacks and whites, middle-class and working-class people are different, but much less different than they are the same. An appreciation and acceptance of commonalities and differences is essential to effective working relationships on the job.

(2) Each of us bears some pain which is the result of historical and cultural forces and the ways we have perceived and interacted with those forces. Rubbing shoulders at work is likely to open old sores and may even generate new wounds.

(3) The development of critical consciousness is related to our capacity and willingness to confront the confusion that arises out of inappropriate stimulus generalization, when stimulus discrimination would be more appropriate. This requires freeing ourselves to confront

consistent experiences and to integrate inconsistent ones in the emergence of self and identity.

(4) Our work-related identities are not distinct from our personal identities. Identity, once established, is not fixed. Although it is shaped by the ways in which we have confronted crises at various stages of development, conditions at work and our perceptions of those conditions can either reinforce current identities or lead us to change (both positively and negatively).

(5) The relationships we establish with others on the job are to a certain extent shaped by our stereotypes of people and positions. These can lead to objectification, when in fact a comprehension of how people deal with difficulties (e.g., displacement, repression, denial, sublimation and so on) might yield understandings that lead to more satisfying, fair and productive working relationships.

YOUR ADDITIONS

(6)

(7)

(8)

(9)

(10)

NOTES

1. Steve Burghardt describes a similar situation, only this time the worker mistaken for a janitor was Black. He was devastated by his own response to the incident. It was as if he had never excelled in school, never earned his MSW. He was thrown into a panic by the experience, feeling that he did not "deserve to be a professional," that beneath it all, he was still what he and others expected him to be—a "hewer of wood." I am also indebted to Burghardt for much of the discussion in this chapter of becoming in tune with one's own pain and for the vignette in which Yolanda responds to her supervisor's sexism.

2. You will recall from Chapter 1 how important Ali's hospitalization and other benefits are to her.

REFERENCES

Allport, Gordon W. (1960). *Personality and social encounter*. Boston: Beacon Press.

Arguello, David. (1984). Minorities in administration: A review of ethnicity's influence in management. *Administration in Social Work,* Fall.

Arsenault, Andre, & Dolan, Shimon. (1983). The role of personality, occupation and organization in understanding the relationship between job stress, performance and absenteeism. *Journal of Occupational Psychology,* Winter.

Babab, Elisha, Birnbaum, Max, & Benne, Kenneth D. (1983). *The social self: Group influences on personal identity*. Beverly Hills, CA: Sage.

Belle, Deborah. (1982). *Lives in stress: Women and depression*. Beverly Hills, CA: Sage.

Bourne, Bonnie (1982). Effects of aging on work satisfaction, performance and motivation. *Aging and Work,* Winter.

Bronfenbrenner, Uri. (1958). Socialization and social class through time and space. In E. E. Maccoby, T. M. Newcomb, & E. L. Hartley (Eds.), *Readings in social psychology*. New York: Holt, Rinehart & Winston.

Brousseau, Kenneth R. (1978). Personality and job experience. *Organizational Behavior and Human Performance, 22*(2).

Bruner, Jerome S. (1956). Freud and the image of man. *American Psychologist,* Winter.

Burghardt, Steve. (1982). *The other side of organizing: Resolving personal dilemmas and political demands of daily practice*. Cambridge: Schenkman.

Clark, Kenneth B., & Rainwater, Lee. (1966). Crucible of identity: The negro lower class family. *Daedalus,* Winter.

Cookey, Charles H. (1902). *Human nature and the social order*. New York: Scribner.

Davis, Larry E. (1983). Racial composition in the agency. *Social Casework,* Fall.

Erikson, Erik H. (1963). *Childhood and society*. New York: Norton.

Erikson, Erik H. (1968). *Identity, youth and crisis*. New York: Norton.

Fanon, Frantz. (1966). *The wretched of the earth*. New York: Evergreen Press.

Faver, Catherine A. (1984). *Women in transition: Career, family and life satisfaction*. New York: Praeger.

Freud, Anna. (1936). *The ego and mechanisms of defense*. New York: International Universities Press.

Friere, Paolo. (1972). *Pedagogy of the oppressed.* New York: Seabury Press.

Garland, Howard, & Smith, Gail Berwich. (1981). Occupational achievement motivation as a function of biological sex, sex-linked personality, and occupation stereotype. *Psychology of Women Quarterly, 5*(4).

Gary, Larry. (1984). *Black men.* Beverly Hills, CA: Sage.

Goldburg, Leo, & Breznitz, Schlomo (Eds.) (1984). *Handbook of stress.* New York: Free Press.

Goodman, Paul. (1956). *Growing up absurd.* New York: Knopf.

Grier, William, & Cobbs, Price. (1968). *Black rage.* New York: Basic Books.

Havighurst, Richard J. (1973). Social roles, work, leisure and education. In C. Eisendorfer & M. P. Lawton (Eds.), *The psychology of adult development and aging.* Washington, DC: American Psychological Association.

Heilbrun, Alfred. (1981). *Human sex-role behavior.* New York: Pergamon Press.

Herbot, Theodore, & Yost, Edward. (1978). Women as effective managers—A strategic model for overcoming barriers. *Human Resources Management,* Spring.

Howe, Louise Kapp. (1978). *Pink collar workers.* New York: Avon Books.

Koumm, Abraham K. (1970). Towards a hypothesis of work behavior. *Journal of Applied Psychology,* January.

Krueger, David W. (1985). *Success and the fear of success in women.* New York: Free Press.

Langer, E. J. (1969). *Theories of development.* New York: Holt, Rinehart & Winston.

Lewin, Kurt. (1948). *Resolving social conflicts.* New York: Harper.

Malcolm X. (1965). *Autobiography.* New York: Grove Press.

Masi, Dale A. (1981). *Organizing for women.* Lexington, MA: Lexington Books.

Maslow, Abraham H. (1970). Self actualization and beyond. In *Motivation and personality* (2nd ed.). New York: Harper & Row.

McNeely, Roger L. (1984). Occupation, gender, and work satisfaction in a comprehensive human services department. *Administration in Social Work,* Summer.

Millet, Kate. (1970). *Sexual politics.* New York: Doubleday.

Mossholder, Kevin, Bedeian, Arthur G., & Armenakis, Achilles. (1981). Role perceptions, satisfaction, and performance: Moderating effects of self-esteem and organizational level. *Organizational Behavior and Human Performance, 28*(2), 224-235.

Neugarten, Bernice L. (Ed.). (1968). *Middle age and aging.* Chicago: University of Chicago Press.

O'Reilly, Charles III. (1977). Personality-job fit: Implications for individual attitudes and performance. *Organizational Behavior and Human Performance,* February.

Pazy, Asya. (1985). A developmental approach to variability in experience of self. *Journal of Humanistic Psychology,* Spring.

Pfeiffer, J., & Lawler, J. (1980). Effects of job alternatives, extrinsic rewards, and behavioral commitment on attitude toward the organization: A field test of the insufficient justification paradigm. *Administrative Science Quarterly, 25*(1).

Powell, George, Posner, Barry, & Schmidt, Warren. (1984). Sex effects on managerial value systems. *Human Relations, 37*(1).

Rogers, Carl. (1970). *On becoming a person.* Boston: Houghton Mifflin.

Rogers-Rose, LaFrancis. (1980). *The black woman.* Beverly Hills, CA: Sage.

Rossi, Alice (Ed.) (1974). *The feminist papers.* New York: Bantam Books.

Row, Alan J., Bennis, Warren, & Bovisarides, James. (1984). "Desexing decision styles." *Personnel,* January-February.

Seybolt, John W. (1976). Work satisfaction as a function of the person-environment interaction. *Organizational Behavior and Human Performance, 17*(1).

Skinner, B. F. (1971). *Beyond freedom and human dignity.* New York: Knopf.

Unger, Rhoda Kesler, & Denmark, Florence L. [Eds.] (1975). *Woman: Dependent or independent variable?* New York: Psychological Dimensions.

Watson, J. B. (1924). *Behaviorism.* New York: Norton.

Weil, Marie (1983). Preparing women for administration: A self-directed learning model. *Administration in Social Work,* Fall/Winter.

Williams, William Julius. (1981). The black community in the 1980s: Questions of race, class and social policy. *The Annals,* March.

Chapter 3

CLIMBING THE LADDER AND
CROSSING THE BRIDGE
Careers in White, Blue, and Pink

Harvey Marcus was feeling good about things. He often did, these days. Only last week, he had successfully negotiated a contract with the state whereby the All-Families Service Center would take primary responsibility for the establishment of group homes throughout the county. It would be the responsibility of his department to subcontract with other providers, train their staff, and see to it that high standards of service to clients would be met. His own staff, he felt sure, was up to the task.

Harvey had just finished meeting with the staff to discuss the implications of the new contract, and he was pleased with the way things had gone. Like himself, the others were relatively young, energetic and committed to their work. It was a closely knit group. Not that they partied together after work; Harvey never encouraged that. But he did favor the sharing of tasks and collective participation in job-related problem solving. Harvey encouraged others to take risks, just as he was willing to do himself. And he motivated them to try out different ideas, no matter how outlandish they might at first seem. He hated the cliché sound of it, but he really did believe that "nothing ventured, nothing gained."

Harvey didn't demand personal loyalty, but he did expect commitment to the job and concern for those who were the ultimate beneficiaries of the agency's work. And his role modeling paid off; there were no clock watchers on his staff. The others felt that they were co-workers, not subordinates, although they all understood who was the boss. They also felt that what they were doing was worthwhile, and they gained a great deal of satisfaction from knowing that their efforts paid off. There was something special about working with Harvey. He wasn't always the easiest guy to work with—sometimes he was so far ahead that it was hard to catch up—but the faster he moved, the more rapidly his staff did, too. No two days at the office were ever quite the same. If you liked a challenge, you liked working with Harvey Marcus.

If one were to trace Harvey Marcus's personal history, one might find some clues to his effectiveness and his style. In fact, if one were to ask Harvey what had shaped his personality and choice of career, he'd answer without hesitation: "My folks and my teenage and early college experiences." One of his earliest recollections was attending an outdoor Pete Seeger concert with his parents. "I used to go to sleep to Pete Seeger and Woody Guthrie records," he recalls. "My dad was a labor organizer and my mother was a teacher. When my father's friends were over, the discussions were always political. They were always into righting some wrong. My mom was a little more conciliatory. Like when I had friends over, if I was too bossy, she never hesitated telling me to be more understanding and let the other fellow initiate some of the play activities.

"My childhood was pretty normal, I guess. Music lessons, afternoon Hebrew school, sports. I was into just about everything: Little League baseball, hockey, and soccer. When I got to high school, though, sports were beginning to take second place. By this time I was involved in all kinds of social, religious, and political activities of my own. I was active in the synagogue youth group (even went to Israel one summer), the debate team, all kinds of anti-war, civil rights, and ecology movements. The big push in civil rights, of course, was over. The year I started high school, we were celebrating the fifth anniversary of the march from Selma to Montgomery. A cousin of mine had been killed in those years. You might remember Goodman, Chaney, and Schwerner, three civil rights workers, two whites and a black, who were murdered and then dumped in a ditch on their way to do volunteer work with the SNCC. Well, Goodman was a distant cousin.

"Anyway, by the time I was a senior, I was president of just about everything. In fact, there was an article on me in the local press almost every other week. And I knew that my dad was proud of the things that I was doing. I think I was getting carried away with myself. The one memory that stands out the strongest was when Mitch Nelson, head of the teen program at the Y, asked me who I thought I was really helping with all the activities I was engaged in.

"I got real defensive. I started telling him about the importance of all the causes I was into, and all the good we were doing. 'What happened to Maggie Pierce?' he asked me. 'Wasn't she supposed to arrange for the bus to take the kids down to the state capitol?' 'Sure,' I replied. 'But I waited three weeks for her to get the information. I had even given her the phone number and the name of the person to call to find out what the costs were in each of two bus companies. So, when she didn't do anything, I did it. Somebody had to.' 'That's just the point, Harv,' he replied. 'You thought the work had to be done and you had to go ahead and do it. But what about Maggie? She hasn't had all the organizing experience you have, and maybe she's not so assertive. Don't you think you might have helped her feel like she accomplished something instead of feeling that she failed, that she let you down? Somebody who really cares about the other person might have gone with Maggie to the telephone and stood there, even helped her dial, supporting her as she made the contact and got the information. You think of yourself as a leader. What do you think real leadership is about: causes, people, or glory?' I was stunned, not sure of what to think.

"But I did think about it, a lot. In fact, I've thought about it ever since. Mitch was the first social worker I ever met. He was a real role model. In retrospect, I suspect that I went into social work because of him. Otherwise I might have gone into labor organizing or even politics. He helped me to realize that if you want to help others, it's not just the big picture but the little guy, your friend, your colleague, the person you work with, that counts too."

When Harvey graduated high school, he took a year off "to find my roots, to find myself. But I wasn't sure where to look. I knew it wasn't in my father's brand of 'secular messianism.' He and his union buddies were still talking about building some kind of just society here on earth, but mostly they were involved in labor negotiations and union contracts. I didn't think the unions were where it was at. I spent about six months working on a kibbutz in Israel, and for a while I thought I had found my place. I was doing something with my own people, and that felt good. But I guess I'm too much a product of 'the fleshpots of Egypt.' "

Harvey wandered about Europe a bit, returned to the States, and enrolled at the university, "like I was supposed to." Majoring in history and journalism, he continued his activism in a number of student organizations. But it wasn't enough. "Reporting on the news wasn't living it." So Harvey spent a year as a VISTA volunteer working in a Chicano community center in south Los Angeles. "I thought a lot about the opportunities that I had had, and the lack of opportunities for the kids with whom I worked. They often expressed an anger that was turned inward, leading to despair and heavy drug use. There was something beautiful and warm in their families and in their tradition, but they just didn't see it. Whenever I found myself unsure about how to intervene, I thought back about how Mitch, at the Y where I grew up, might have acted. And suddenly one day I woke up and I realized that I wanted to be a social worker."

* * * * *

If we were to interview the other workers at the All-Families Service Center, we'd uncover different histories, but we might also uncover similar patterns of personal development and career choice. In this chapter, we'll examine five theories of career development. The discussion will be grouped under various categories: (1) *trait-factor theories* (in which individuals' capabilities and interests are matched with vocational opportunities); (2) *self-concept theories* (which trace the development of more clearly defined self-concepts as individuals grow older, and which match those concepts to the opportunities available); (3) *personality theories* (in which job or career choices are perceived as efforts to satisfy personal needs); (4) *opportunity theory* and career choice (in which circumstances, generally outside the individual's control, contribute to career choices); and (5) *developmental approaches* (which parallel some of the conceptual frameworks described in Chapter 2). We'll look at the first three approaches together, then move on to the fourth and fifth. Finally, we will examine how different individuals act out their career alternatives and pursue alternative life choices within the agency setting.

TRAIT, PERSONALITY, AND SELF-CONCEPT THEORIES

Almost three decades ago, John Holland, a researcher from Johns Hopkins University, proposed that the adequacy of a person't occupational choice (i.e., the closeness of fit between the individual and the occupation) is largely a function of the extent to which the person is knowledgeable about the self as well as about occupational alternatives. Now this may not be startling information, but Holland's subsequent work generated some interesting propositions. It was Holland's contention that people have different traits and that these emerge gradually over time, leading to relatively appropriate or inappropriate educational and experiential decisions which then have implications for occupational choice. Holland speaks about six kinds of orientation:

(1) Those with a *realistic* (motoric) orientation tend to seek concrete rather than abstract problem situations, scoring high on traits such as concreteness, physical strength, and masculinity, and low on social skill and sensitivity. They avoid tasks involving interpersonal and verbal skills. They might be found to predominate in such occupations as engineering and truck driving.

(2) The *investigative* (intellectual) orientation aims at organizing and understanding (thinking) rather than dominating or persuading (acting), and tends to be more asocial than sociable. Scientific researchers and many academics tend to share these characteristics.

(3) The *social* (supportive) orientation, in contrast, tends to characterize people who seek close interpersonal situations (for example, teaching, social work, and therapy).

(4) The *conventional* (conforming) orientation is typified by a concern for rules and regulations, strong identification with power and status and, frequently, subordination of personal needs. Persons with these traits seek work situations where structure is either readily available or where they can participate in the development of rules and procedures that regulate interpersonal interactions. Accountants and systems analysts tend to fit this pattern.

(5) An *enterprising* (and frequently persuasive) orientation tends to characterize persons in the business and corporate world, where power, the domination of others, the manipulation of forces and status are central to success. But there are entrepreneurial types in the human services as well.

(6) The *artistic* (aesthetic) orientation is manifested in strong self-expression and in the establishment of relationships to others

through artistic endeavors (music, writing, and so on). People with this orientation may share asocial characteristics with the investigatives but tend to be more feminine than masculine, expressing emotion more readily than other people.

Now, you might assume that most social workers tend toward the social and supportive orientation, and you'd be quite correct. Of the six staff persons we've met thus far, only Carl, a non-social worker, doesn't seem to possess much of this trait. You might identify him as conforming and conventional. In Chapter 6, you'll discover that he is also artistic—but not necessarily at work. Reexamine what you know about Harvey Marcus. Clearly he, like most of us, reflects a number of traits. He is enterprising, investigative, and, to a certain extent, realistic. We already know that Millicent is strongly social in her orientation, but that she is also artistic. Ali is both social and conventional. How would you describe Yolanda? Do you know enough about Sam to identify his most characteristic traits? What about yourself? Undoubtedly you possess some of each of these traits.

How would you rank the traits of others with whom you work: your supervisor, subordinates, the agency administrator, other colleagues? You might want to use the test you just devised to find out. To what extent might such ranking help you understand what leads them to behave in the ways they do? What trait differences might lead to some interpersonal conflict between members of the staff? Clearly, no one's traits are carved in stone, and many of us tend to express one or more of these to a lesser or greater extent at different stages in our lives and in our work careers.

Harvey's personal history illustrates this point. Moreover, Harvey has chosen to act out his work life at the agency so as to be able to find expression for a number of different traits. In that he is quite fortunate. Both his occupational choice and the conditions in the agency and its environment permit him to capitalize on a number of different traits simultaneously. Is this true also of the other staff members at the agency? Is it true of you in your work setting? To what extent does the environment in the agency in which you are employed limit your opportunities to express these traits? Has this environment shaped them somewhat differently, so that you have come to change the order of the hierarchy? Has it caused you to emphasize some traits over others in response to the expectations and reward systems in the workplace?

* * * * *

Exercise 3.1

Hierarchy of Traits

1. Take the six traits we have described (*realistic, investigative, social, conventional, enterprising,* and *artistic*) and list them in hierarchical order, reflecting those that you think most strongly characterize *you*. (Top to bottom reflects high to low.)

   (1)_____

   (2) _____

   (3) _____

   (4) _____

   (5) _____

   (6) _____

2. If you are not sure of an order, design an exercise that may help you decide. First, list five work-related responses that reflect each of the six traits. I'll get you started.

   "When I first started to work at the agency, I
   (1) reorganized things in my office to make things more attractive and aesthetic (*artistic*).
   (2) set out find out how things work, who is responsible for what, and what resources were available to me (*investigative*).
   (3) asked around about rules and norms, read the procedures manual (*conventional*).
   (4) introduced myself and got to know my co-workers informally by meeting with them both in their offices and outside at coffee and lunch, etc. (*social*).
   (5) checked out the pecking order, finding out who makes what decisions and how (*enterprising*).
   (6) walked around, checking on the layout, equipment (computers and filing systems) (*realistic*).

   Now add 24 more items (five per trait). Look over the scoring instructions for **Exercise 1.5.** Create a similar form for this exercise, with six columns. Take the test and score yourself.

Lofquist and Dawis have described the work adjustment process as one in which a person's flexibility reflects the degree to which one can tolerate a lack of correspondence between the work environment and one's own personal character traits. The more one can tolerate a lack of correspondence, the more flexible the individual. On the other hand, some people become active in attempting to alter the work environment so as to increase its correspondence to their personality styles. Clearly, Harvey is among these. Some people change their place of employment when blocked in the expression of one trait or another. Yolanda, you will recall, worked in the GM plant, which had required investigative and enterprising skills with which she had not been comfortable. For Millicent, the conventional and conforming requirements of her earlier life as a nun and a teacher in a parochial school had become stifling. As she matured, she found an increasing need to express herself artistically, persuasively, and intellectually. What changes have you observed in your own behavior over the years?

Davis and others have used questionnaires and statistical methods to generate a "birds of a feather" hypothesis that assumes that members of an occupational group will exhibit increasingly homogeneous personality traits over time. But this is a controversial hypothesis at best. Its major flaw is that it tends to focus on one trait at a time. In fact, Super and Bachrach point out that efforts to define differences in personality traits among members of different occupations is futile because too much overlap exists, and because both occupations and jobs tend to tolerate a wide range of personality differences.

It may, in fact, be more profitable to look for those factors which influence the sequences of career decisions that people make in response to the opportunities that may be offered them. How they deal with those opportunities may, to a large extent, be a factor of the extent to which they are willing to take risks. According to Atkinson, for example, our motivations to achieve and to avoid failure have a great deal to do with the extent to which we are willing to take risks on the job. Those who seek to avoid failure will frequently set either extraordinarily high or extremely low goals for themselves, whereas those who are influenced more by an achievement motive are likely to aspire to more attainable goals. Thus achievement-motivated people are likely to engage in moderate risk-taking activities.

Fear of failure may increase the likelihood that some people will be willing to consider entering less prestigious occupations. What does this say about Harvey and Yolanda? What does this say about Sam, whose father had been a physician and had expected Sam to follow in his footsteps? Might there be some connection between Sam's selection of social work as an occupation and his (risky) move from Lebanon to the United States? Perhaps it might be more appropriate to assume that risk-taking has relevance to vocational behavior, if not to vocational preference or choice. This might explain why both Millicent and Harvey are willing to take considerable risks in the work they do, and how the ways in which they perform on the job contrast with the relatively low risk of selecting a professional occupation that is fairly well suited to their personality traits and that is not particularly high on the ladder of occupational status.

There is yet another theoretical approach that you might find useful in comprehending career development. It is frequently referred to as "social learning theory" and is associated with the work of John Krumboltz. Like the approaches already explored, it also tends to identify the personal and environmental events that shape individual career decisions. It begins by examining inherent attributes like race, gender, physical type and the traits we discussed earlier. But it focuses more heavily on the environment of the workplace (rules, reward procedures, social and technological environment and so on). In addition, social learning theory concerns itself with the individual's learning history.

Many people tend to learn in an "associative" manner, observing the relationships between events and thereby developing a capacity to predict alternative outcomes (contingencies) as the consequences of alternative actions. Others are more "instrumental" in that they've learned that specific actions are likely to lead to specific outcomes. Some social learning theorists suggest that a person's interests, or the ways he or she acts out career decisions, may be more the outcome of experience than of personality traits. Because outcomes are specific (getting a job, being rewarded for effective performance, moving up the ladder), one learns to adjust one's traits in those directions from which reinforcement is likely to come.

People who are realistic about themselves and the world around them are not likely to act in ways that generate costs that exceed their perceptions of current or future gains. For Yolanda, earning an MSW degree was not particularly risky and was clearly worth the investment, whereas working at GM, despite her earlier expectations, required paying too high a price for the rewards available.

Anne Roe, a clinical psychologist whose early research interests focused on factors that lead to artistic creativity, has also directed investigations toward uncovering the ways in which developmental patterns affected by earlier childhood experiences lead both to career choices and particular ways in which people act out those choices. Like many of the researchers described in Chapter 1, she also concludes that needs that are routinely satisfied do not become motivators, and that higher order needs, in the sense of Maslow's self-actualization propositions, will disappear entirely if they are only rarely satisfied. Lower order needs will become dominating motivators if they are only rarely satisfied, and this may block the appearance of higher order needs. She also concludes, however, that needs that are satisfied after an unusual delay will become motivators when both the strength of the need is great and the amount of delay between arousal and satisfaction is prolonged. This may help to explain the rather radical shift in perspective and behavior on Millicent's part, after some 20 years as a teacher and a nun.

Roe's research also focused on specific child-rearing techniques, particularly the ways in which parents interact with children. She analysed overdemanding, overprotecting, and accepting parental behaviors. *Overprotective* parents tend to make excessive demands on their children, yet they will fulfill and satisfy their physiological needs. However, they may be somewhat less prompt in gratifying demands for love and esteem. Children of overprotective parents learn to place emphasis on the speed with which needs are gratified. Thus, although lower level needs tend to be gratified quickly, higher order needs become more connected to dependency on others and, later in life, to conformity. By definition, *overdemanding* parents make excessive demands on their children, but they also impose conditions on the love offered the child. ("I'll love you if you do this or that.") Thus both overprotective and overdemanding parents are to some extent rejecting their children. In contrast, *accepting* parents tend to gratify their children's needs at most levels.

Roe concludes that children who grow up in an accepting atmosphere are more likely to select one of the helping professions, whereas scientists, engineers, accountants, and others who are not heavily person-oriented in their work tend to come from a home atmosphere where they may have experienced both the coldness and rejection sometimes associated with overdemanding parents. Nevertheless, even these people may choose helping professions if the need for esteem, love and belonging is intense, and if some opportunity for its gratification exists.

Ervin Staub, a psychologist from the University of Massachusetts, has published an interesting book on the biological and social origins of good and evil. Based on extensive interviews, he concludes that there exists a pattern of child rearing that seems to encourage altruism in later years. It requires a warm and nutrient relationship between parent and child in which parents not only espouse altruistic values but also exert firm control over their children. These parents use a combination of firmness, warmth and reasoning, pointing out to children the consequences of misbehavior, as well as of good behavior. They actively guide the child to do good, to share and to be helpful. Staub concludes that children who have been coached to be helpful tend later to be more altruistic when a situation arises in which they can help others.

These are the same children who are likely to select occupations in which they can be helpful to others on a regular basis. Both their self-concept and their social needs are actualized through and in the helping process. Altruistic adults tend to have mothers or other significant caretakers who explained to them the consequences of being hurtful, and who did so with a great deal of feeling. Calm and unemotional admonitions do not seem to produce altruists. On the other hand, children of chronically depressed mothers seem to be particularly sensitive to the distress of other children, and are often preoccupied by it. This preoccupation may also affect occupational choices.

Have we discovered something more about Ali, Harvey, and the others at the agency? About yourself?

BOYS AND GIRLS ARE NOT THE SAME.
NEITHER ARE MEN AND WOMEN

Much of what we've discussed so far has been gender-neutral; that is, we've assumed similar factors to hold true for both boys and girls, men and women. In point of fact, however, boys and girls do grow up differently in our society. The way in which they are socialized leads to differences in adult perception about the self, about one's career and about the best ways to pursue that career. There are, of course, hazards in generalizing from the experiences of a few. Nevertheless, I think the benefits of sharing some of the All-Family Service Center staff's recollections of the childhood experiences that shaped their work-related identities may be worth the risk.

*   *   *   *   *

Ali speaks: "I suppose if I had my druthers, I would have gone to college. Two years at the J.C. (junior college) weren't enough. I might still do it when the kids (her brothers and sisters) are all out of the house and don't need me anymore. But if I were to tell you what I really wanted, it was a normal mom and a normal family life.

"You know, I never had what I thought was normal. For sure, not the TV idea of normal. Like on those family shows they used to have on TV. You know, the mom fixes breakfast for the kids in the morning, the father goes off to work, and the kids go off with clean clothes to school, and the parents are there when the kids need 'em, when they've got a problem. When my mom first was hospitalized, my aunt came over, and she was like that. She came from Cleveland, and she was warm, and she was caring, and she straightened out the house for us. All the rooms were clean and neat for the first time that I could remember. I helped her the way I used to help my mom when she was sick, but Aunt Flora, she was something else.

"She knew just how to get things organized, how to put them in the right places, and how to make everybody feel good about themselves, not only because they had clean clothes, but because they were clean inside.

"My mom had sometimes tried to make us feel important, but we were important only if we didn't make life more miserable for her. I knew I was important because I took care of her. But when Auntie Flora came, I began to feel important 'cause I was me. I realized we could be a family even if my mom wasn't there. My Aunt Flora made me feel I was a good person, and I decided that I would be good.

"That's my main goal in life, to be a good person, to be decent, to be helpful to others. I didn't want my brothers and sisters to feel the pain of my mother's loss. I made sure they always had clean clothes and breakfast on the table. Sure, I'd like to have a college degree, but I don't think a college education is all so important. What's important is to do your work well, to make other people feel good about themselves and to feel good about your own self. I know all this talk about women being as good as men. Sure they are. But we don't have to be off and doing the same as men. What I like most about working in this agency is that women can be women here, I mean the way they should be.

"They're helpful to others. They make them learn about themselves and deal with their own problems. Social work is really all about mothering in the best possible way. That's why I respect Millicent and Yolanda so much. They're good at what they do, and they really care about people. And in my own way I'm good at what I do, too. And people know I care about them."

* * * * *

Yolanda explains: "I used to think I was different, but as I get older I realize how much I've been shaped by the system. I don't mean just because of my black skin. That may be the biggest part, but it's still only part of it. The other part is that I'm a woman. When I was in high school, I was determined not to turn out like some of the others in my neighborhood. My dad worked hard. Too hard. And my momma was a secretary. When she wasn't doing somebody else's work in the office, she was helping us kids grow up to be somebody. My parents always taught me to be the best that I can. They tried to teach my brothers the same thing, but they were defeated by the system, mostly because they were Black. But Black girls didn't have so hard a time of it. Maybe it's because white teachers weren't so scared of us. We didn't have to act macho.

"I tried to excel at everything when I was at high school. I even became a cheerleader. We were known as the T 'n' A squad. That's for 'Tits and Ass' (she laughs). We were supposed to make sure that everybody cheered in support of the team. The boys, after all, were taking the falls, and they were the ones who were going to win and lose for all of us. But we weren't above generating some attention for ourselves. It was our job to get everybody behind the team so that the boys would succeed. That's how it was, and I guess that's how it still is.

"My momma wasn't just a secretary; she organized and kept track of things so that her boss would succeed. And he did. Sure, he moved up and he brought her along with him, but it was always his moves, even if she had been the one to make it possible. You know that old saw: 'Behind every successful man there stands a woman.' Well, that was my momma. My daddy may not have been so successful, but Momma was always there anyway.

"One thing I learned from my momma . . . if you're going to succeed, you'd better work your darnedest at it. If you're good, people will know it. Not that I don't care about my husband. Reggie gets a lot of support from me, and I know it's tough on him, being a Black man and all. But I was determined to make it on my own. When it was fashionable, I wore a dashiki. But I'm no African. And if you're going to make it in America, you got to do it as an American. So after I traded my T 'n' A uniform for a dashiki, I turned my dashiki in for a dark suit. But you know, it wasn't enough. That crack about putting pressure on a woman at GM, that wouldn't have happened to a man. I worked hard on that report, and I worked on it all alone. I think it was really a good piece of work. I wish that I could have discussed it with someone else before turning it in. I'll never know, because I never really got any feedback on it."

* * * * *

Millicent speaks of the influences on her development: "You know, it's funny. It wasn't until I became a 'sister' that I was exposed to some of the lessons that boys learn as they're growing up. When I became a nun, I learned that you didn't have to like everybody else that you interacted with. There were important things to do, and you could do it together with other women. It wasn't easy for us to learn to share responsibilities with people who were so different from us. We were fortunate in having a strong ideology, a religious belief that sustained us. We were also told what to do and how to do it. Boys learn some of these lessons earlier.

"I think back about my brothers. When I was in school, we had one *team* sport—volleyball. Our other sports were all *individual*—swimming, track and tennis. But my brothers played football and baseball. They learned how to be team members early. You didn't have to like the other members of the team, you only had to play with them. If it took five to play basketball, you didn't have to like the other four. And if you needed nine to play baseball, you learned how to get along for the benefit of the team. And if you needed eleven for football, it didn't matter whether they were Catholic or not, smart or not so smart, from one side of the tracks or another. What counted was that the team won. I didn't learn much about winning as a little girl, and I didn't learn much about counting on others or getting along with them even if I didn't like them."

* * * * *

Harvey explains: "When I decided to take this job, it was clear to me that I was either going to be successful—that is, that I was going to be able to make a difference in terms of placement opportunities for people in real need—or I would have to move on to another job, perhaps even another agency. And when I look for other staff for my department, I look for people with similar kinds of concerns. It's only recently that I've begun to realize that some of my attitudes may be sexist. It even feels sexist to be saying this. So let me explain.

"When Mel Stanford applied, what I liked about him was that I saw him as a 'comer.' He knew the kinds of questions to ask, and those questions weren't only about the job itself. He wanted to know what kinds of opportunities there might be for advancement. He was loaded with ideas, and I liked that. And I wasn't kidding myself that he'd stay here forever. But I knew that with people like him aboard, we'd expand the department's functions, and as long as we grew, there'd be opportunities for him to expand his own areas of responsibility as he showed capability and initiative. That's the kind of person I am, and that's the kind of staff I want around me.

"When Billie Jean Elving applied for a job, she came with superb recommendations. She asked good questions, too, but they tended to be about the job as it was currently defined. I think she liked what I had to tell her, because clearly she wanted to make a contribution to others. Billie Jean was looking for self-fulfillment on the job, for an opportunity to do important things and to do them well. I was sure she would. But I was equally certain that without a great deal of support, I couldn't expect her to take initiative for expanding the department's functions. When I asked her what she wanted out of her career, she looked blank. And then she responded: 'We're not talking about my career, are we? I can tell you what I want out of this job: an opportunity to do something worthwhile.'"

* * * * *

Harvey Marcus may have hit on a difference in the way in which men and women approach their careers, a difference that he was not quite ready to put into words. This difference is discussed more fully in a study by Margaret Hennig and Anne Jardim. In it, they describe their interviews with 100 successful women managers. Their conclusions are worth summarizing, as they may help to provide some insight into the comments made by Ali, Yolanda, Millicent and Harvey.

Hennig and Jardim conclude that men and women respond to both jobs and careers in ways that reflect different habits of thought. For example, women tend to respond in the present, describing their jobs in terms of the activities they perform and as a means of support, or a contribution to the family's earnings. They tend to see their careers as reflecting an opportunity for personal growth and self-fulfillment, and as a way of achieving personal satisfaction while making a contribution to others.

Men, on the other hand, see jobs in the context of *now* and *later,* simultaneously. Men tend to visualize a career as a series of jobs, a progression leading to greater recognition and reward. For men, jobs seem to be part of a career, whereas women separate the two issues completely, with the job being viewed as something that exists in the here and now, and a career being perceived in an intensely personal light.

Perhaps this has to do with early socialization in which girls learn to separate personal from career goals. In attempting to satisfy their own and society's perceptions of a woman's role, there is for some an intense pressure to succeed so well at the woman's role that no one might question their mastery of it. Only when they are secure in this role are they free to pursue occupational goals. But when they are free, they attempt to do it all. This has sometimes been referred to as the "supermom" syndrome. It also results in women switching off and on different persons, with one person on the job and another at home. Such an approach may explain the complex of feelings that Yolanda is experiencing (see Chapter 2). It may also help to explain why Ali has, in effect, turned the office into a home in which she clearly fulfills what she perceives to be an appropriate female role. We might suspect that Yolanda knows a great deal more about Reggie's job than he does about hers, and that she may even think about her own work as a job, and about his work as a career, limited as it may be within the context of the opportunities available to him at the plant.

Hennig and Jardim also talk about differences in the personal strategies pursued by men and women. Men tend to ask, "What's in it for me?" thus bringing the future into current consideration. In contrast, women tend to think more about how they will be judged in relation to their current work. The personal skills drawn upon for that work will also be different for men and women. Boys' sports are team sports, as Millicent observed, in which winning is important and in which individuals suppress feelings in order to make their contributions to the team. Boys learn this on the playground, on the street and in team activities at school.

Girls, in contrast, have few parallel experiences. The prestigious sports for them tend to be tennis, swimming, golf, gymnastics and skating—one-on-one sports in which winning and losing may be less important than how one plays the game. Technique becomes important, while strategy takes second place. For adult women, this may lead to an inordinate emphasis on performing well in the here and now, based on the assumption that promotion, if it comes, will be a recognition for competence. This is essentially a passive approach.

For men, on the other hand, getting ahead may depend on how well one works as a team member. Promotions may depend as much or more on how one gets along with others as on the extent to which one performs competently. The "old boy network" continues to be important. It is probably exploited by knowing how to relate effectively to others, to make important contacts, to be recognized for one's contributions and to use such recognition for being delegated additional responsibility.

CAREER FROM A DEVELOPMENTAL PERSPECTIVE

These notions are supported by the work of Donald Super, who proposed that vocational self-concepts develop on the basis of children's observations of and identification with adults. He concludes that a person's mode of adjustment in one period of life is likely to be predictive of techniques used to adjust in later periods.

While it is possible for an adolescent's identification with a significant other to lead directly to an educational or vocational decision,[1] it is more likely that this identification will lead to a chain of events that might not have occurred otherwise, and that may have significant vocational implications. Harvey reflected this in his recollection of the influence of a social worker at the Y.

Super's life-stage theory of vocational and career development suggests that people progress from an exploratory stage in which they test various alternatives and even undergo trial work experiences (like Sunday school teaching, volunteering, working in VISTA or testing out an alternative career like newspaper reporting), and then make a commitment. These experiences lead people to seek training, which in turn leads to the emergence of a new identity. The nature of that identity may be different for women than for men because of both different societal perceptions and differences in one's own self-perception.

Super's work is complemented by that of Ginzberg and his associates. They perceive vocational choice as an irreversible process characterized by a series of compromises between wishes and possibilities. It begins with a fantasy period in which the individual (generally a child) thinks of himself or herself as a movie star, a millionaire or a fireman. This leads to a tentative period in which interests, capacities and values are explored in the context of life chances and opportunities.

Having reached the point of understanding personal likes and dislikes, the young adult achieves some understanding of his or her capacities. Tempering these with personal and social values, each person begins to explore ways to implement tentative choices. This is the beginning of the realistic period in career choice. It leads to a crystallization based on the exploration of a number of alternatives. Ginzberg assumes that this realistic stage occurs at the age of 18-22, but as we have seen, as new opportunities present themselves, even mature adults can continue their explorations, often changing their perceptions of both self and opportunities.

Murphy and Burck have suggested that a midlife developmental period should be added to Super's stages. They argue that when as many as one out of five physicians express dissatisfaction with their careers, when so many women are entering income-producing careers after having raised families and when more and more people are exploring alternatives in their 30s, 40s and even 50s, a new notion of development may be necessary.

Regardless of earlier successes, they suggest, it is not uncommon for people in mid-adulthood to experience a decrease in self-esteem, to question the meaning of their own lives and to reexamine their personal values as a part of an overall process of stock taking. The attainment of a certain amount of economic success may be accompanied by the realization that even achieving one's earlier career objectives is no longer fully satisfying. Moreover, once children have left the home and are no longer dependent, the availability of new opportunities leads to a reactivation of one's search for a close fit between values, interests and capabilities. Golumbiewski observes that midlife career transitions increasingly occur between the ages of 35 and 45. Some people at this point experience a great deal of torment as they examine from whence they have come and conclude that they have not arrived at any place worth being. A colleague of mine has a sign on his door saying, "I got there, but I don't know where I'm at."

Midlife transition involves a disparity between one's achievements and one's aspirations. "I'm tired of being owned," another colleague of mine recently admitted. "I want to be my own person." And this from a university professor, who presumably has more "academic freedom" to pursue his own interests than might be the case for most people in our society! For those who are successful in becoming their own man or their own woman, a career change in midlife may result in a horizontal rather than a vertical move. Fortunately, this does not necessarily require starting out all over again. After all, how often can one scale Mt. Everest?

Both Yolanda and Millicent made lateral (horizontal) career shifts. Of the two, Millicent's was clearly the more radical. For Yolanda it entailed moving from the private sector to the voluntary sector, but she remained in social work. Millicent continued in her role as an educator, but the shift from working with children in a parochial school to counseling adults in a family services agency required a radical transformation in her identity and her perceptions of the world. For her, the Church no longer provided clear guidelines for occupational progress or personal identity. She expressed and acted on a need to reassert control over her own self-development. She chose not to passively follow a course of action set in motion years earlier. Although age tends to be negatively correlated with risk taking, for her, dissatisfaction with life as she had come to know it required a new process of self-testing, a new period of training and a new set of responsibilities in a different institutional environment.

All three women quoted in this chapter expressed different responses to the occupational stereotypes developed as children. Although all three continue in sex-stereotyped occupations, personality factors and self-perceptions have influenced the way in which they act out their career decisions. All three not only desire to work, but need to. And all chose occupations in which the opportunity for achievement was clearly present.

OPPORTUNITY AND CAREER CHOICE

Throughout this chapter we have accepted the likelihood that external circumstances, including chance and opportunity, have a significant impact on both occupational choice and the outcomes related to such choices. In contrast with the psychologists whose work we have examined in some detail, it is probably fair to suggest that most sociologists would argue that being at the right place at the right time may have a greater impact than character traits, personality or other developmental factors. Osipow concludes that to many psychologists, "chance" represents an irritant to be minimized so that better decisions might be made and events brought under the control of the individual.

In contrast, sociologists are more likely to focus their attention on external variables, those forces that are generally outside of the individual's control or over which the individual may have only minimal control. Thus social forces like the economy, societal attitudes and prejudices and chance meetings or acquaintances—in effect, "the throw of the dice"—may have more to do with where one ends up occupationally than many of the variables discussed here.

In the mid-1950s, Theodore Caplow documented the rigid limits on the variety of career choices available to some members of society, leading him to conclude that for some, occupation is hereditary. Hollingshead's famous study of *Elmtown's Youth* provided an earlier foundation for the conclusion that social class and occupational aspirations were closely connected. So far, we haven't said much that would suggest any major disagreement with the conclusions arrived at by the psychologists discussed above.

However, Peter Blau and his associates have provided a conceptual framework that places the occupation and its position in society more centrally in the line of vision. Blau suggests four characteristics of occupations and individuals that should be considered as key factors in career choice:

(1) the individual's occupational information and the available information on that occupation;

(2) the individual's technical qualifications and the functional or technical task requirements of the job or occupation;

(3) the individual's social role characteristics and the nonfunctional
social and institutional requirements of the occupation; and

(4) the individual's reward value hierarchy and the amounts and types of
status, financial or intrinsic rewards offered by the occupation.

Let's take the first item. The amount of information an individual
may have about a particular occupation, job or career choice may be
less dependent on his or her innate abilities or developmental history
than on the extent to which society provides information about the
occupation or career, and the extent to which the occupation or
profession in question is successful in making itself known to potential recruits. Second, jobs change, occupations grow technically and
professions expand in their knowledge and technological bases. As
they do so, they require members with specific competencies and
capacities.

These requirements may not always be as technical as they seem.
For example, the rapid growth of programs aimed at minority groups
and the poor in the 1960s and 1970s required social workers who were
not only sensitive to the needs of the oppressed but whose own
experiences were similar. Social work undertook an intensive effort to
recruit minorities to graduate schools, and when this was not possible
indigenous personnel were recruited and trained as paraprofessionals. Many went on to earn Associate of Art degrees in the human
services. The civil rights movement and Affirmative Action programs
likewise increased occupational and career opportunities that were
directly linked to "protected" minority status.

The political activism characteristic of that period made social
work a particularly attractive profession for those who were themselves politically active. It provided them with career opportunities in
community organizing, social planning, policy development and politics itself.

Clearly, however, activism is not the major draw to social work.
We've already said a good deal about the current identification of
social work in the public eye as a female occupation. Thus those
whose social role characteristics tend toward the helping and the
nurturing are more likely to select an occupation that not only supports but requires such behavior. Finally, occupations such as social

work may be limited in the financial rewards and the social status or prestige that they can confer on their membership. However, they are high in other rewards: belonging, self-actualization and self-fulfillment. This is particularly true for those who possess the appropriate trait hierarchy (refer to your own self-assessment in **Exercise 3.1**). Nevertheless, the extent to which social work and other careers in the human services provide you with the opportunity to actualize and fulfill yourself may be more a factor of the occupation itself than of those traits.

CAREER STYLE AS A FUNCTION OF ORGANIZATIONAL STYLE

Clearly, work and careers are integrally related. The place where you work is the arena within which career decisions and moves are often made. If *careers* refer to the stages and levels of occupational growth and development, the *arena* refers to the place where the action takes place. That action can be within a social agency, where most social workers are employed, or in the larger community or field-of-practice arena (for example, community mental health, substance abuse or aging). In each of those arenas there may be opportunities for upward or horizontal mobility. Upward mobility generally refers to movement either into managerial or specialist levels within an organization or else out of the organization into a more responsible job. Such moves are frequently accompanied by an increase in responsibility and autonomy, better pay and working conditions and more prestige. They may also be accompanied by more pressure and job stress. Large agencies, particularly those with tall hierarchies in which there are many levels of management, or those in which there is a high ratio between managers and subordinates, afford the greatest opportunity for upward mobility.

For many professionals, however, upward mobility is not a goal. Among my own colleagues at the university, for example, I would find few professors aspiring to become deans or university presidents. Most of us, in fact, shy away from becoming department heads because it would take us away from our direct relationships to students and from our cherished free time to do scholarly work. Most schoolteachers do not aspire to become principals, and most social workers value direct practice, moving only reluctantly, sometimes with more than a few protesting kicks, up the occupational ladder. Many, in fact, might define upward mobility in terms of increased skill and competence. The job title may not change, but recognition of such competence by colleagues, both within the agency and outside, is perceived as advancement. For many, movement into a managerial role would be diverting at best and would more likely be perceived as requiring considerable sacrifice.

For many human service professionals, lateral mobility might be much more appropriate. As we noted earlier, this was the case for both Millicent and Yolanda. For some social workers it might mean a shift from treating individuals to working in family treatment, or from community work to protective services. Such shifts may entail some retraining but rarely require downgrading in terms of salary and benefits.

Large agencies that provide a wide variety of services or that serve many populations and cover multiple geographic locales also provide considerable opportunities for lateral moves, as do smaller agencies that are in a growth or expansionary phase of development or that shift their programs and services in response to new needs and opportunities. Examples include women's crisis centers and home health care services for the disabled. In some of these settings, in fact, workers may be expected to shift jobs or perform multiple jobs at a moment's notice. Such agencies generally have flat structures, with few or no levels of hierarchy between practitioners and top management.

Anthony Downs,[2] a social scientist with the Urban Institute, describes five career styles common to most complex organizations, each of which is a different response to change (Downs, 1967). I think you will find his analysis instructive and recognize both yourself and many of your colleagues and supervisors within it. He refers to "climbers," "zealots," "advocates," and "statesmen." Before we examine each of these, one at a time, I want to point out that these categories tend to deal primarily with upward mobility within an organizational setting and thus are too limited to serve as a framework for analysis of all aspects of organizational careers. Nevertheless, they do provide some important insights into why people behave as they do in social agencies and other work settings.

The "climber" is on the move up, hopefully, to the top. There are a number of ways in which he or she can get there. The most direct is promotion. One way to improve the odds for promotion is to be recognized as competent at carrying out one's official tasks. Another is to get involved in as many committees and subgroups as possible.

If the chances for promotion are relatively small, the climber may resort to aggrandizing his or her area of responsibility. This strategy is often perceived by others as empire building. The more resources under the climber's control, the more influence he or she has within the organization and the more indispensable the climber becomes. The surest way to build an empire is to increase the number of personnel directly under one's control. As the number of subordinates increases, added staff must be justified by absorbing more programs and responsibilities. These may come either from areas previously controlled by other people or from new programs generated by the climber.

When the path to promotion is blocked and when empire building is not feasible, the only route left for a climber may be to jump to another agency, selling personal skill, expertise, and confidence. The only real constraint here is the job market. If there are no jobs available for the climber and all possible contacts made during the empire building process have been tried, then the climber's path may be blocked. The response is often frustration that may be expressed in interpersonal conflict.

In terms of leadership style, the climber tends to closely control subordinates to ensure nobody else is seen as a rising star. This style of leadership often suppresses innovation from below. Nevertheless, the climber believes, rightfully so, that the more change there is, the greater opportunity for advancement of subordinates as well as himself or herself.

The second type is the "conserver," who in many ways is the opposite of the climber. Like climbers, however, conservers tend to be concerned mainly with themselves. Unlike climbers, conservers strive to maintain the status quo. They are very much against any change that would threaten the relatively secure position they presently occupy. They prefer to be told exactly what to do so that they will not be blamed for any possible mix-up. Conservers supervise their subordinates closely in order to prevent innovation that might upset standardized and tried procedures and policies. In short, you may recognize the conserver as the typical bureaucrat.

The "zealot" is very stubborn and believes he or she knows what is wrong with, or what is best for, the agency or one of its client populations. Win or lose, zealots fight the good fight, always on the side of right. Typically, they have a high energy level. The ability to fight all odds continuously and still maintain enthusiasm is precisely their strength. For these reasons, zealots become excellent change agents. They are often effective in the start-up of a new program or a new agency. Unfortunately, the same degree of innovation is not expected of subordinates. Loyalty to the zealot is.

The "advocate" is a person who has exceptionally high commitment to the goals of the organization or department of which she or he is a member, or to a client population serviced by the agency. Great pride is taken in the accomplishment of the agency's or department's service goals. The organization advocate has two major skills: the ability to protect his or her part of the organization against all external threats—hence in a budget meeting, for example, he or she will fight to get the most for her or his agency; and the ability to mediate conflict within his or her department or organization. The combination of these two skills makes the agency advocate the person likely to be promoted to the head of an organization. The client or consumer advocate does the same for those with whom he or she is concerned. In doing so, consumer or client advocates are more likely to be in conflict with others in the agency. Consumer advocates are not as likely to head a service agency as are agency advocates.

All advocates use what can be called a situational approach to leadership. Hence, innovation is encouraged when appropriate and discouraged when superfluous.

The "statesman" tends to be more concerned with the welfare of society as a whole than with the agency or a particular client population. Regardless of the impact on the organization, the statesman will do what he or she *perceives* to be in the best interests of society. Unlikely to devote much time to performing detailed, day-to-day activities, the statesman spends a good deal of time developing overall plans and objectives. Statesmen do well in public relations type situations or any area that interfaces with clients or the public at large. When backed up by managerial staff who are zealots or advocates, they make good agency administrators, but not when left on their own.

* * * * *

Exercise 3.2

Career Patterns

Downs writes of five career styles: climbers, conservatives, zealots, advocates, and statesmen. Next to each of the staff persons listed below, indicate the designation(s) you think most clearly characterizes their styles.

Yolanda Stephenson   _____   _____
Samich Mansouri   _____   _____
Alberta Schmid   _____   _____
Millicent Kapinski   _____   _____
Carl Farrell   _____   _____
Harvey Marcus   _____   _____
Yourself   _____   _____

1. None of us are limited to a single style. Morever, our styles may change at different stages in our occupational careers. What would it take to shift Carl from his current style to that of a climber or statesman?

2. If you've identified any of the staff members as zealots, under what circumstances might they become climbers, advocates, conservatives or statespersons?

3. If you've identified any of the staff members as advocates, are there circumstances in which their behavior might shift to that of climber, zealot, conservative or statesperson?

4. It's no secret that you identified Harvey as a climber. Do you think he'll be so identified throughout his career? Why? Why not? Substantiate your answer on the basis of what you already know about Harvey and what you know about career and occupational development from having read this chapter.

REVIEW AND TENTATIVE CONCLUSIONS

Blue collar, white collar and pink collar careers are different. So are the factors that lead people to making career choices and that lead to career opportunities.

(1) Trait theory postulates that a combination of innate and developmental factors leads to different personality traits which, in turn, correlate closely with occupational choice and with the ways in which people perform on the job. Single traits by themselves may not be a determining factor, but combinations of traits, when perceived in hierarchical order, are very often decisive.

(2) Learning theorists suggest that career choices may be more the outcome of experiences than of personality traits. Learning is associative and instrumental, and what people make of what they have learned is likely to have a significant impact on who they try to imitate and on their selection of work-related alternatives.

(3) Child-rearing practices and early socialization lead to self-perceptions which in turn lead to career choices.

(4) Boys and girls do not grow up in the same society, and not all siblings grow up in the same families. What they learn about teamwork and how they come to evaluate themselves may not only lead to specific career choices but may also affect the ways in which they perceive both jobs and careers. For men, the two seem to be closely interrelated. For women, jobs and careers may be perceived separately; the latter taking on a distinctly personal character.

(5) Recent findings by those relating life-stage approaches to career development suggest that people move through a process that includes fantasy, testing and trial work, training and commitment. But commitment may not be a forever thing. Increasingly, people take stock at midlife, and this reevaluation may lead to significant career

and occupational shifts, particularly when new opportunities present themselves.

(6) "Closeness of fit" between the individual and the occupation or job may be related to characteristics of both, including: knowledge and information, skills and technical requirements, social role characteristics and reward-value hierarchies.

(7) Within any organization, people develop career styles, some of which may change as the individual becomes older or as the length of service increases. Typical styles include: climbing, conserving, zealotry, advocacy and statesmanship.

YOUR ADDITIONS

(8)

(9)

(10)

(11)

(12)

NOTES

1. Recall that both Sam and Harvey decided on social work at least in part on the basis of certain experiences with social workers who served as role models, and

that Ali was much influenced by her aunt, who took over when her mother was hospitalized.
2. The following ten paragraphs are taken from Lauffer (1984).

REFERENCES

Atkinson, J.W. (1957). Motivational determinants of risk-taking behavior. *Psychological Review,* Summer.

Barnet, R. C. (1975). Sex differences and age trends in occupational preferences and occupational prestige. *Journal of Counseling Psychology,* January.

Baruch, R. (1966). The achievement of motive in women: A study of implications for career development. Unpublished doctoral dissertation, Harvard University, Cambridge, MA.

Blau, Peter, Guspad, Joseph W., Jessor, Richard, Parnes, Herbert S., & Wilcok, Richard C. (1956). Occupational choice: A conceptual framework. *Industrial Labor Relations Review,* July.

Burlin, F. D. (1976). Locus of control and female occupational aspirations. *Journal of Counseling Psychology,* January.

Caplow, Theodore. (1954). *The sociology of work.* New York: McGraw-Hill.

Chernesky, Rosyn. (1983). The sex dimension of organizational process: Its impact on women managers. *Administration in Social Work,* Fall/Winter.

Clark, E. T. (1967). Influence of sex and social class on occupational preference and perception. *Personnel and Guidance Journal,* Winter.

Collins, Eliza G. (1982). Stepping out of glass slippers. *Harvard Business Review,* March-April.

Davidson, Marilyn, & Cooper, Gary. (1983). *Stress and the woman manager.* Oxford, Eng.: Martin Robertson.

Davis, James A. (1964). *Great aspirations.* Chicago: Aldine.

Dawis, Robert V., & Lofquist, Leonard H. (1976). Close personality style and the process of work adjustment. *Journal of Counseling Psychology,* January.

Doughtie, E. B., et al. (1976). Black/white differences on vocational preference inventory. *Journal of Vocational Behavior,* January.

Downs, Anthony. (1967). *Inside bureaucracy.* Boston: Little, Brown.

Farshan, Barbara L., & Goldman, Barbara H. [Eds.] (1981). *Outsiders on the inside.* Englewood Cliffs, NJ: Prentice-Hall.

Form, William H., & Miller, Delbert C. (1951). *Industrial sociology.* New York: Harper & Row.

Francesco, Anne Marie, & Hakel, Milton D. (1981). Gender and sex as determinants of hireability of applicants for gender-typed jobs. *Psychology of Women Quarterly, 5(5),* Supplement.

Ginzberg, E. (1972). Towards a theory of occupational choice: A restatement. *Vocational Guidance Quarterly,* Spring.

Ginzberg, E., et al. (1951). *Occupational choice: An approach to a general theory.* New York: Columbia University Press.

Golumbiewski, R. T. (1978). Mid life transition and mid career crisis: A special case for individual development. *Public Administration Review,* Summer.

Harmon, L. W. (1970). Anatomy of career commitment in women. *Journal of Counseling Psychology,* January.

Hennig, Margaret, & Jardim, Anne. (1977). *The managerial woman.* New York: Doubleday.

Holland, John L. (1973). *Making vocational choices: A theory of careers.* Englewood Cliffs, NJ: Prentice-Hall.

Hollingshead, A. B. (1949). *Elmtown's youth.* New York: John Wiley.

Holloway, Stephen. (1980). Up the hierarchy: From clinician to administrator. *Administration in Social Work,* Winter.

Kadushin, Alfred. (1958). Determinants of career choice and their implications for social work. *Social Work Education,* April.

Kerson, Toba, & Alexander, Leslie. (1979). Strategies for success: Women in social service administration. *Administration in Social Work, 3*(3), Fall.

Korman, A. K. (1966). Self esteem variable in vocational choice. *Journal of Applied Psychology,* Winter.

Korman, A. K. (1970). Towards a hypothesis of work behavior. *Journal of Applied Psychology,* January.

Kravitz, Diane, & Austin, Carol. (1984). Women's issues in social service administration. *Administration in Social Work,* Winter.

Krumboltz, J. M. (1979). A social learning theory of career decision making. In A. M. Mitchell et al. (Eds.), *Social learning theory and career decision making.* Cranston, RI: Carroll.

Lauffer, Armand. (1969). *Social actionists come to social work.* Ann Arbor, MI: University Microfilms.

Lauffer, Armand. (1984). *Understanding your social agency* (2nd ed.). Beverly Hills, CA: Sage.

Leibowitz, Zandy B., Farran, Carla, & Kaye, Beverly. (1980). Will your organization be doing career development in the year 2000? *Training and Development,* February.

Lipsett, L. (1962). Social factors in vocational development. *Personnel and Guidance Journal,* Winter.

Lofquist, Leonard H., & Dawis, Robert V. (1969). *Adjustment to work.* Englewood Cliffs, NJ: Prentice-Hall.

Lyles, Marjorie A. (1983). Strategies for helping women managers. *Personnel,* January.

Murphy, P., & Burke, H. (1976). Career development at mid-life. *Journal of Vocational Behavior, 9,* 4.

Osipow, Samuel H. (1983). *Theories of career development* (3rd ed.). Englewood Cliffs, NJ: Prentice-Hall.

Patti, Rino, et al. (1979). From direct service to administration: A study of social workers' transitions from clinical to management roles. *Administration in Social Work, 3*(3), Fall.

Roe, Anne. (1956). *The psychology of occupations.* New York: John Wiley.

Roe, Anne, & Klos, Donald. (1969). Occupational classification. *Counseling Psychologist,* January.

Sarason, A. (1977). *Work, aging and social change.* New York: Free Press.

Slocum, William L. (1965). Occupational careers and organizations: A sociological perspective. *Personnel and Guidance Journal,* December.

Staub, Ervin. (1985). *Altruism and aggression.* New York: Columbia University Press.

Super, Donald E. (1957). *The psychology of careers.* New York: Harper & Row.

Super, Donald E., et al. (1963). *Career development: Self concept theory.* New York: CEEB Research Monograph No. 4.

Super, Donald E., & Bachrach, P. B. (1957). *Scientific careers and vocational development theory.* New York: Teachers College, Columbia University.

Chapter 4

CLAIMING PROFESSIONAL STATUS
Professionalism, Semi-Professionalism, and Deprofessionalization

Sam was in a quandary. The staff meeting had gone all wrong. He knew he was somehow to blame but wasn't sure of what he could or should have done differently. There had always been some misunderstanding about the New Americans Project, but he had just not expected such vituperous opposition to his proposals. At first Sam had felt personally attacked; then he became defensive about both his ideas and his clients.

Sam had proposed expansion of the project in both scope and the number of clients to be served. In a well-documented memorandum distributed before the meeting, he had shown (to his own satisfaction) that the funds available through a federal grant and state support could be used more efficiently by building on the strengths of the family and network structures that existed in both the Arab and Southeast Asian communities. His proposal was straightforward.

By reducing the number of professional social workers and public health nurses assigned to the project, it would be possible to employ a larger number of people from within both communities. These paraprofessionals would perform both outreach and counseling functions. Their involvement, he reasoned, would have several advantages over the current operation of the project: (1) The new Americans, with some training and guidance, would be employed in meaningful tasks, thus facilitating their integration into American society. (2) Because they knew and understood the needs of the populations from which they themselves had come, paraprofessionals would be able to more readily identify people with special needs for which the agency was equipped to provide service. (3) As persons culturally indigenous to these populations, they would provide an effective communication link between the agency and the new Americans.

Sam understood that his proposal would have to be accepted by the department heads at the agency. That's how things operated. Decisions to move into new program areas or to modify long-standing operating procedures were always made consensually, in open dialogue among colleagues. He knew he would have to substantiate whatever claims he made about efficiency or the improvement of services. He was prepared for this. But he was not prepared for the overwhelmingly negative response generated by his paper. "What makes you think that people who have been in this country only for a year or two, perhaps no more than a few months, could possibly take on the professional chores of assessment, treatment and referral?" someone had challenged. But this was not exactly what Sam had proposed.

"We've always prided ourselves in our commitment to confidentiality. If you are right that these people network among themselves, how can you expect them to maintain professional confidences? Wouldn't some of your clients find it difficult sharing personal information with others who are so much like themselves, perhaps no more competent to deal with the problems presented than the clients themselves?" someone else had asked. "These people need all the help they can get and that we can give them," a third had volunteered. "Let's not treat them any differently or with less respect than we would our other clients. They deserve and they need the best professional service."

"Building a volunteer core within each of these communities, yes. But professional help and volunteer involvement are different than turning over responsibility to paraprofessionals. I saw enough of this," another staff member offered, "in the Model Cities[1] program to know that paraprofessionals are likely to organize themselves into a distinct political force. That may have been OK for Model Cities, but this isn't a political agency. We are professionals providing a professional service."

Only Millicent Kapinski had supported his ideas, and even then with some reservation. "Sam's ideas have considerable merit," she had argued. "We should not dismiss them out-of-hand without some further thought and careful analysis. Let's look at what he's really proposing: involving members of the client population in service delivery and needs identification, finding more effective ways of communicating with people whose language skills and lack of familiarity with our institutions make it difficult for them to accept and utilize services, and increasing our outreach and ultimately the numbers of clients served at no cost to the agency. Those are worthwhile goals. But the mechanisms he is suggesting are different from those we employ in our other departments. So let's not reject the goals so quickly, let's examine the mechanisms and the alternatives we might find to them." The meeting had ended on this note of both consensus and disagreement. "OK, so Millicent saved my skin," Sam thought, "but where do I go next?"

THE TRIUMPH OF PROFESSIONALISM

What Sam Mansouri first perceived as an attack on himself, then on the populations for whom he had responsibility and finally on the plan he was proposing was perceived by other staff members as an appropriate defense of professional standards. Professions like social work deliver services, generally advice or action, to individuals, organizations and larger institutions, to groups of people or to the public at large. Professional services, it is generally assumed, are supported by esoteric knowledge systematically developed and applied to client problems. This knowledge may be substantive or theoretic, based on cumulative experience, experimentation and observation. Generally, it is a mixture of all three. Professionals claim that their practice should rest on such knowledge and that they are competent to apply it to problems by virtue of their study and apprenticeship under those who have mastered that knowledge.

When we think of a "real pro," we often have in mind someone who is skilled, competent in the application of knowledge, dedicated and devoted to others, and consistent in his or her professional behavior. To a large extent, this is because professionals, as Everett Hughes[2] has pointed out, *profess* to know better than others the nature of matters within their occupation's domain. Such matters include the causes or consequences of certain behavior and the techniques or technologies that might be used to influence behavior or ameliorate conditions considered negative for certain classes of people. They also profess the right to apply those practices and areas of knowledge to people in need. Sometimes professionals attempt to claim an *exclusive* domain; that is, they demand and often receive the exclusive right to practice in prescribed ways and with certain people. Well-established professions, like medicine and law, have been largely successful in receiving support from the general public for such claims of exclusivity.

People acting in their professional capacities are expected, even required, to think *objectively* about matters that others might deal with on the basis of less systematized knowledge, more limited intellectual exploration, greater sentiment or emotion and often with fixed and rigid points of view. Because professionals do profess to be skilled and qualified, they ask that they be trusted. They may even demand that clients share with them secrets that are related to the problems being dealt with. In turn, they commit themselves to confidentiality and to the use of those secrets only in the best interests of the client. This demand for trust has yet another consequence.

Many professionals claim that only others similarly initiated in knowledge and practice can effectively judge whether a professional's performance is both skilled and ethical. For example, physicians consider it their prerogative not only to define the nature of disease and health but also to determine how medical services ought to be distributed and paid for, and the criteria by which medical practice is to be evaluated. They resist efforts by non-physicians to define any of these issues. Similarly, social workers not only develop technologies like case work, community work, case management and specially tailored approaches to supervision but also engage in actions aimed at affecting public policy. In turn, policy affects both types of practices and the services available to populations in need. Thus, while professions like social work are themselves products of social change (new knowledge and emergent technologies, and modifications in the ways in which risks are shared and services are provided as a consequence of industrialization and urbanization), they also attempt to shape the forces that lead to their own growth and the expansion of the services they consider essential to the well-being of others.

What this requires is a certain amount of solidarity, a commitment to professional values and norms, an ideology that espouses concern with populations at risk, a willingness to share a common fate and a sense of trust in other members of the profession. While members of some other professions and occupations may be expected to be equally committed or competent, members of the general public, even of the populations served, are not equally deserving of trust. Nor is the expression of commitment by such publics likely to be accepted as a substitute for competence.

Many social workers are at pains to prove that their work cannot be done effectively by amateurs (untrained or even partially trained people involved in interventions on the basis of commitment or good will). This is an understandable defense of professionalism. It took at least two generations of practitioners, trained at universities, before professional social work practice was distinguishable from the volunteer friendly visitor and the social actionist or reformer. Although social work underwent a period of "deprofessionalization" in the mid-1960s and early 1970s, in which paraprofessionals and others were involved as nearly full-fledged social agency team members, and in which the professional degree was downgraded from the MSW to the BSW, in the 1980s social work has again to focus inward, determined to deepen knowledge and improve skill.

Some professions, social work included, may not be as successful in substantiating their claims or in winning exclusive rights to perform what they profess. Claims of competence from multiple sources may lead to competition between different professions for clients, for the right to perform certain services and for status, prestige and material rewards. But such claims also lead to cooperative endeavors and joint efforts. Because social work is in many ways among the least exclusive of professions, its success is largely dependent on the ability of social workers to establish effective linkages with other occupations and community resources. Moreover, social workers accept the involvement of clients in decision making and other actions as a basic point of philosophy and an essential ingredient to their technology. These characteristics notwithstanding, a strain toward exclusivity, in social work remains nevertheless, as it does in all professions.

With this background in mind, let's return now to Sam and his situation.

* * * * *

Exercise 4.1

Objections to Change on the Basis of Professionalism

Based on the foregoing discussion, identify as many separate reasons for objections to Sam's proposal as you think might have motivated the others at the staff meeting. Describe these briefly, in a sentence or two.

1.

2.

3.

4.

5.

6.

7.

8.

Harvey Marcus had been sitting quietly throughout the meeting. Part of him had been straining to defend Sam's proposal, but the better part of valor, he felt, was to keep his counsel to himself. "There are better ways of handling this," he thought. Based on what you know about Harvey, what do you think he had in mind?

As supervisor of clinical services, Yolanda Stephenson was convinced that Sam's approach was totally in error. You have probably already guessed at some of the reasons and have jotted them down in the exercise. But Yolanda didn't object to Sam's goals as articulated by Millicent. She just didn't think that Sam's approach was appropriate to this agency, and she had made that point clear at the staff meeting. But she felt for Sam. Her earlier, private outburst at the New Americans program was behind her, but her sense of propriety and of professional prerogatives was strong. If she were to meet with Sam privately to discuss her feelings, what are the issues she would raise?

You already have a good idea of where Millicent stands. You know enough about her background and experiences in Chile to have a good sense of how she regards involving people in comprehending their situations and acting on their comprehensions. But Sam's proposals trouble her, too. Look over the list of objections you jotted down in **Exercise 4.1**. On which of these does she base her reservations?

Share your ideas with others who are reading or have read this book. Do they agree with your assessments in **Exercises 4.1** and **Exercise 4.2**? On which points? Where is there disagreement? Now put these ideas aside for the moment, and let's reexamine what else we know about professions and professionalism. We'll then go on to consider the roles of paraprofessionals, volunteers and clients in an agency's "human resource mix."

UNDERSTANDING PROFESSIONS, PROFESSIONALISM, AND PROFESSIONALIZATION

Professionals think of themselves as being different from other occupations, and to a large exent they are. We're not talking here about absolute differences; we're talking about differences of degree. These differences are reflected in:

(1) a *general and systematized body of knowledge* that the profession considers exclusively its own;
(2) a commitment to the *communal or public welfare*, in contrast with the more private interests of the individual members of a profession;
(3) a perception that an occupation has not only a right but a duty to be *self-governing and autonomous* in its determination of appropriate practices;
(4) a claim to a *jurisdiction of certain problems* (and certain publics or clients) over which it should have *authority*;

Exercise 4.2

Resolving the Contradictions

Knowing what you know about Harvey, Yolanda and Millicent, consider how each might help Sam reconsider his proposal so as to resolve the contradictions between the dominant staff point of view and the ideas in Sam's proposal.

1. Harvey's ideas:

2. Yolanda's ideas:

3. Millicent's ideas:

---

(5) a distinctive *occupational culture* replete with its own folkways and relationships, one that is *recognized* as distinctive by the general public.

Social workers, like other professionals, argue that they have a body of knowledge that has been systematically and rigorously developed through scientific research and practical experience. This body of knowledge, it is further claimed, can be taught and applied to practice, that is, to social intervention with individuals, groups, communities and the larger society. This knowledge base, of course, is not exclusively that of social work. It has, to a large extent, been borrowed from psychology, sociology, political and economic science and the practical experiences of other allied professions (medicine, law, urban planning, education and others). Nevertheless, its organization, the way in which components of the knowledge base are integrated with each other, as the professional claims, is exclusively that of social work.

Like other professionals, those in social work postulate that the transmission of knowledge requires an elaborate and formal system of training. Some of that training, for beginning-level competence and skill, can be conducted within a bachelor's level degree program. More advanced knowledge, however, must be transmitted through a master's (MSW) or a doctoral training program that may lead either to a DSW (doctor of social work) degree or to a more theoretic and research-based Ph. D. The location of these basic educational programs in a university setting is important.

It is argued by most professionals that if such training were to be non-academic, it would be less than professional. Academia, it is assumed, ensures that the knowledge transmitted to students is both theoretically sound and generalizable. In contrast, the knowledge base of other occupations, where the training may not be university-based, would tend to be more practical and limited. Further, the systematic knowledge of professional training, it is presumed, discourages the inconsistencies and lack of integration in the knowledge base that are found in some nonprofessional occupational groupings. It is no wonder that some professionals might fear that the transmission or transference of their knowledge to others who are less than fully professionally trained may result in inconsistent, ineffective and perhaps even dangerous practices.

Staff members at the All-Family Services Center have an image of their organization as being highly professional in its orientation. "When we started the adoptions and foster care unit," the agency's director had written in a paper prepared for the regional conference of the Child Welfare League, "we decided to recruit the *best trained staff* available, and then to provide them with additional training opportunities. Besides assigning some of our more experienced workers to the unit, we recruited young MSWs from Columbia, Michigan, and Wisconsin—schools with top-notch reputations as educational institutions and places where faculty members were reputed to be national leaders in child welfare because of their contributions to research and theory development. But even then we weren't satisfied. We sent two of the staff people to intern in the State of Oregon's Permanency Planning Project, where new knowledge and new approaches were being tested to make sure that kids would no longer be bounced around the foster care system without any hope of ever being permanently located with a family that cared about them. And our unit supervisor participated in the Project CRAFT[3] training at Michigan.

"In the long run," he concluded, "this training paid off in the professional quality of our work and in the effectiveness of our staff." It had additional pay-offs as well. The agency's reputation as a "professional place to work," and as an organization with high professional standards, was bolstered by the fact that there were frequent opportunities for staff members to continue their professional education, both through in-service training and through opportunities to attend conferences and participate in university-based courses and workshops.

In addition to their emphasis on a *knowledge base*, professionals also view themselves as being *community-conscious*, performing a public service rather than serving private interests. By contrast, when unions talk about better pay, better working conditions and more worker involvement in setting agency policy, they are reflecting private, not public, interests. Thus members of any profession will tend to distinguish the concerns of their professional associations from those of unions and protest movements, even unions of professional workers. "Professionals have no business unionizing," Millicent had argued at an organizing meeting called by a local affiliate of the American Federation of State, County and Municipal Employees. "Our work should be directed toward the best interests of the child, the best interests of the disabled and the best interests of the isolated elderly."

I don't mean to suggest that all social workers or all members of other human service professions feel the same way. In many places, social workers, nurses, teachers and others *are* unionized. In fact, teachers' unions and the professional association to which teachers belong are often one and the same organization. The National Education Association and its state affiliates often function as professional associations at the state and national levels and as unions at the local or organizational level. Interestingly enough, the demands presented in contract negotiations—for example, more educational leaves for teachers, better pay and working conditions and smaller teacher/student ratios—are almost invariably phrased as being in the public interest, since the education of children is improved by improving the relationship between teachers and children and the quality of teachers' competence and skills.

The differences between professions and other occupations are perhaps more a matter of degree than of substance. The *norm of altruism* exists in varying degrees in all occupational groupings, but professionals justify their claim to altruism in several ways. First, they establish *codes of ethics* that are intended to symbolize their commitments and to serve as the standards against which practitioner behavior is judged. Second, they claim to involve students and in-

itiates in a long socialization process that includes professional training in an academic setting, as well as various forms of internship
under experienced and certified practitioners. Finally, they do, on
occasion, disbar or decertify their practitioners for unethical practices, generally defined as activities that are clearly aimed at the
disadvantage of the populations they are serving while increasing the
advantage for the practitioner in question. Agencies are considered to
be more "professional" to the extent that they adhere closely to
ethical standards and to appropriate norms of behavior.

This *self-regulating behavior* is the justification frequently cited
for the claims made by many professionals that they should be relatively free of external control. Many professions demand a license to
perform their activities as they see fit. What they attempt to do, in
effect, is to carve out areas in which members can only be evaluated
by their peers. They do this by engaging in self-study, establishing
standards for practice and, frequently, establishing certification programs that are intended to ensure competent practice. Some may
even distinguish between levels of practice. Further, they recognize
exceptional practice through a variety of awards. Your local NASW
(National Association of Social Workers) chapter undoubtedly offers
a "social worker of the year" award and may further divide that award
into "advocate of the year," "clinician of the year," "administrator of
the year" and so on. Each of these represents a cherished professional
value or role.

A more objective evaluation of professions and professionalism,
however, shows little evidence that professional autonomy contrib-
utes to high standards of professional service. There are some who
argue that ethical codes are not set up to protect the welfare of the
clients, but instead serve to conceal the activities of the profession
from public examination by permitting none other than fellow professionals to penalize those who violate the norms.

The growth of the consumer movement in the United States has led
to closer scrutiny by the public of the activities of various professions.
The increase in both private and public action suits against individual
practitioners (as well as the organizations that employ them) for
malpractice has forced some professions into stricter self-
governance, as well as greater acceptance of limits on their autonomy.
Often these limits are imposed through state and local licensure
procedures. Nevertheless, professions have had considerable influence in establishing the standards that are passed into law. For example, national associations and their state and local chapters frequently

design model legislation which serves as the basis for licensure. In many cases, public commissions are set up to review examinations that professionals are required to pass to receive certification. Generally, however, these bodies are composed to a large extent of members in good standing within the profession itself.

Some professions are more successful than others in staking a claim to a particular turf, thus acquiring a mandate to serve a specific client population, deal with defined problem areas and apply technologies for which they are especially suited and their members effectively trained. But they may not be alone in staking those claims. Other occupational groups may make counterclaims. Thus far, no occupational group has successfully challenged the legal profession's access to the courtroom, although individuals may be permitted to act in their own defense.

The medical profession continues to maintain hegemony over health care services, but not without some challenge from nurses and allied medical professionals who claim both the competence and the right to perform certain tasks that have previously been performed only by physicians. Clinical psychologists and social workers have also made significant headway in wresting authority from psychiatrists over certain client populations. For example, whereas at one time only those clients treated under the direction of a psychiatrist might be eligible for reimbursement through third-party payments (i.e., insurance payments), today social workers may be permitted the same privilege.

Further, what was once referred to as the "medical model" has been challenged as inappropriate to social work and other human service occupations. This model might be stated as follows: The physician, by dint of training and experience, is both more knowledgeable and competent to determine appropriate treatment, based on careful and scientific diagnosis. Proponents of the medical model argue that if clients were to be treated as consumers rather than as patients, determining what service or what treatment they wished to buy, they would be likely to receive poorer service, often making the errors inherent in lay versus professional judgments. Perhaps the appropriate word here is not "consumer" but rather "customer."

Professional services, by definition, are not like the products offered in a department store or cafeteria. Customers are expected to evaluate their own needs and judge whether the investment is worth the outcome. Patients are not. "The customer is always right" may be appropriate to the purchase of consumer goods, but it is totally inappropriate, from the perspective of the medical model, when it comes to making judgments about complex, life and death matters that only a competent professional can decide. Not only has consumer activism led to a challenge to this model, but the very nature of medical practice has produced the need to involve patients in decisions. Indeed, active support of the patient may be necessary in many forms of treatment (especially in areas where mental health or chronic illness are involved).

Social work, in contrast, has always given at least lip service to the involvement of the client in determining his or her needs and in selecting from alternative ways to deal with the problems for which service has been requested. The ethos of a "client's right to self-determination" is central to both the social worker's statement of professional ethics and to many of the technologies involved in enabling people to "help themselves." Nevertheless, elements of the medical model are found throughout social work practice. Remember, we are referring only to models. In the real world of practice, no profession fully reflects the characteristics of a single model.

The pure medical model is not to be found anywhere, since clients always have considerable power over professionals. In hospitals as well as social agencies they may, through their participation in committees and boards (representing the public), even have the power to hire and fire professionals. Those going to private practitioners have the power to cease attending and to select another practitioner if they so desire. If the uncontested authority of the professional ever existed, it clearly does not at the moment, nor is it likely to in the future.

Revelations of professional abuse and malpractice have led to accusations of elitism and of a lack of concern for or commitment to the welfare of clients in favor of the pursuit of financial gain (in contrast with the professions' claims of being community-conscious). Clients have become increasingly sophisticated consumers of professional services, and this sophistication can be traced to the expansion of formal education, the availability of client-focused books that demystify medical and other practices or that assist in individual self-help, the growth of self-help groups that compete with and/or cooperate with professionals, the attention of the mass media, and the growing activism of women's groups, blacks and other minorities, as

well as certain functional categories of consumers (ex-mental patients, parents of the developmentally disabled, adult adoptees, and
others).

PROFESSIONS AS COMMUNITIES AND CULTURES

You have undoubtedly heard or run across the term "professional
community." Not all professionals have a sense of themselves as part
of a community, but many do. Members are bound by a common
identity based on common values, clearly understood role definitions,
relatively clear boundaries, the power of reproduction (via the transmission of culture to succeeding generations) through schooling and
internships and, to a certain extent, a common language (what we
refer to as "professional jargon"). The community includes formal
professional organizations like the AMA or the National Association
of Social Workers, colleges and training schools, the organizations or
agencies in which professionals work (like social agencies or human
service organizations), as well as all kinds of informal groupings
within the profession. These groups include participants involved in
social and legislative action, and others involved in a variety of
leadership roles. These leaders are the role models who epitomize in
their behavior the competencies and attitudes that the profession
values.

Professions, like other communities and cultures, have their own
distinctive histories. And like their counterparts, they tend to be
selective about what and whom to include in those histories. Social
work in the United States traces its roots to the settlement house
movement and the progressives of the 1860s and 1880s. Early heroes
and heroines include Stanton Coit, who established the University
Settlement in New York, and Jane Addams, who established Hull
House in Chicago. The Charity Organization Societies of the 1870s
were established to coordinate the work of myriad private, mostly
voluntary social services for the poor. Theirs was a humanitarian
response to the urban poor who were ill, jobless, inadequately
housed and/or exploited. Their activities included both legislative
and advocacy efforts which led to the establishment of juvenile courts
and child welfare reforms. At the same time, the COSs applied
"scientific methods" to service coordination and referral.

In the mid-1920s, Mary Follett and Edward Lindemann were leaders in the community movement that pioneered efforts to organize

Exercise 4.3

Professionalism and Your Agency

How "professional" is your agency? Based on your observations, to what extent are each of the characteristics of a profession also characteristic of your agency (high, medium or low)? Is this appropriate? How would you change or modify the situation?

	High, medium, or low	Is this appropriate?	What should be changed?
1. Practice is built on a systematic body of *knowledge*.			
2. Practice is oriented toward the community welfare (*altruism*) in contrast to the private interests of staff.			
3. The agency and its staff have consider- able *autonomy* over the nature of its programs, the population served and the way it provides these services.			
4. The *authority* of the host profession's culture and profes- sional collegial relationships have precedence over bureaucratic or organizational demands.			

> In balance, would you say that the agency is "too professional" or "not professional enough"? Please justify your answer in terms of the norms of knowledge, altruism, autonomy and authority we have been discussing.

primary groups in communities where people lived. They promoted the establishment of cohesive social units that would assume responsibility for themselves and guide their own destinies, and in so doing ensure the expansion of democracy. In the 1930s and 1940s social workers not only assumed leadership for the growth of America's social welfare programs but developed or adopted new technologies that led to more effective clinical and group practices.

I have mentioned a few of social work's heroes and heroines, its founding mothers and fathers. But professions may also have their villains. In today's political climate, Ronald Reagan and Reaganomics are pictured as villains. Thus history and folklore combine to help professionals define who they are like (and who they are not like). It can be dangerous for an individual member of a profession to identify with a villain or to agree with many of a presumed villain's notions or policies.

Professional culture has a considerable impact on the growth of a professional community. To a large extent, this stems from the development of *colleagueship* within each professional group. All occupations establish certain formal and informal criteria for membership inclusion. They also legislate, generally informally, the form and extensiveness of the relationship to established between fellow members.

There are rites and obligations of colleagueship, both in theory and in practice. We have already noted that in most professions only one's colleagues are presumed to have the right to judge whether one has practiced ethically and effectively. For this reason, colleagues must be able to take each other's sentiments for granted. They must be able to communicate freely and openly among themselves and to share confidences that could not be repeated to uninitiated ears. Even the rules of confidentiality, those that limit the sharing of information outside "the fraternity" or "the sorority," are frequently waived with one's colleagues.

Colleagues share what Everett Hughes has called "guilty knowledge." This is a private knowledge shared only among colleagues through the subtle use of argot or jargon. For example, a psychiatrist can say shocking things about patients in technical terms to fellow psychiatrists which they would never share in lay terms to lay people. Other physicians will use black humor in the operating room but would never consider sharing the same jokes with a patient's family or even with members of the hospital's board of directors.

Trusting their colleagues, fellow professionals can say things to each other in such ways that they feel confident they will be comprehended and accepted. Their jargon is more than scientific; it is an assurance that what they intend to convey will be properly understood by others.

CLAIMING THE RIGHT TO BE TRULY PROFESSIONAL

You've probably observed that some occupations are "more professional" than others, or at least are so perceived by their members and the public. On what basis are such perceptions founded? One might be defined as "sociological," a second as "historical" and a third as "political." In the sociological approach, different occupations are contrasted on the basis of the extent to which their attributes approximate the norms discussed (altruism, knowledge, autonomy, and authority).

Using the historical, or process, approach, we might say that an occupation has become a profession when the following have occurred: (1) it has a name that is clearly identifiable to its own members and to the public at large; (2) its members are organized into a professional association that sets standards, establishes and maintains a code of ethics and provides advocacy not only for its members but for the welfare of the public at large and the particular populations that the profession serves; (3) it has one or more professional schools, generally university-based, through which knowledge is developed, codified and transmitted; and (4) it is recognized as a profession by law, through processes that include both licensure and certification and the exclusive (though sometimes shared) right to perform certain tasks, serve specified populations or use a designated set of technologies.

The third approach to determining when an occupation has become a profession is more clearly political. From this perspective, professions are distinguished from other occupations in that they are more successful in convincing the general public that their claim to mandates should be honored to the partial or total exclusion of other occupational groups. There seem to be three sources of such political power. The first is *timing*. Some occupations were simply there earlier and have been around for a longer period of time. Thus physicians, the military and the clergy have long-standing claims to professional status.

The second source of power stems from the extent to which a profession deals with high levels of *uncertainty*. By this I mean the issues that they handle which clients feel incompetent to handle by themselves. In earlier times, when problems seemed to be less complex or when solutions were less technical, it may not have been as necessary to have so many specialized professions. A *shaman* or medicine man could deal with health, mental health, and even political issues. Today, however, we need a wide variety of health and mental health professions, political scientists, economists, legal specialists, and others to deal with the ever-increasing complexity created by uncertainty.

This uncertainty doesn't have to be intrinsic; it can be artificially produced. For example, in the guise of providing clarity, some consultants have mystified organizational processes so as to increase the demand for their services. Attorneys have mystified divorce, thereby artificially creating an area of uncertainty over which they exercise considerable control. Whether by accident or collusion, accountants have created such complexity in the tax laws as to make their services (to some of us, at least) indispensable.

A third source of power is *indeterminacy*. There is an interesting paradox to be found in the fact that many of the things that professionals do are not explicitly defined, and are in fact largely indeterminate. Thus psychiatrists, family therapists, and social work clinicians involved in direct practice with clients are expected to have wide latitude in their choice of action and the judgments they make. The problems presented are so complex, however, that it is not easy to break down the required responses into step-by-step procedures. In contrast, the determination of eligibility for public welfare assistance can easily be broken down, much as one would break down the steps in an assembly line procedure. For this reason it is not necessary to hire professionals to do eligibility determinations.

Family treatment, by being defined as indeterminate, requires the competence of a trained professional who can be expected to behave on the basis of relevant knowledge and with adherence to an ethical code. What makes this so paradoxical is that the very inability to codify information and procedures in certain areas of practice is the basis for claiming authority over those areas. And yet professional knowledge is presumed to be not only transmittable but codifiable.

Does this in some way help to explain the reluctance of the All-Families Service Center staff members to employ paraprofessionals for work with the New Americans Project?

SOCIAL WORK AS A SEMI-PROFESSION

Amitai Etzioni, a sociologist from Columbia University, has classified occupations along a continuum based on the extent to which they have been successful in their claims for designation as full professions. His analysis suggests that the internal attributes of professionalism are much less influential in laying claim to professional status than the issues pertaining to political power. Etzioni's continuum looks like this:

(1) Historically *established professions*—physicians, college professors, clergymen, lawyers and engineers;
(2) *New professions*—natural scientists like biologists and chemists, and social scientists like economists and sociologists;
(3) *Semi-professions*—nurses, social workers, librarians and teachers;
(4) *Would-be professions*—accountants, personnel managers, funeral directors, chiropractors, pharmacists and business executives;
(5) *Marginal professions*—lab technicians, insurance agents, medical technicians and others generally given "paraprofessional" status.

Our concern here will be with the *semi-professions,* particularly social work.

Social work—like nursing, library science, and teaching (at the secondary and elementary school levels)—is not merely classified as a semi-profession but as a *female* semi-profession. Women make up approximately two-thirds of the social work profession, four-fifths of the library profession, 85% of those involved in teaching elementary school, and virtually 98% of those practicing nursing. This is not the only reason that these occupations have been sex-labeled, however.

For a wide variety of reasons, women have been locked into a relatively small number of occupations. Their identification with the semi-professions is particularly apt in terms of stereotypic gender and sex-role characteristics. Women are expected to be in occupations in which their performance is to support the role of males (for example, nurses in relation to physicians). They are also presumed to be caring, oriented toward helping and toward providing succor (social work). Moreover, they are expected to provide child care at home and, by extension, in the classroom (teachers). There may even be some similarity between their responsibilities for home-making (including the storing, categorizing, and dispensing of food) and similar work performed in libraries (where they do much the same to information).

Against this background, it is not difficult to understand why social work and the other female occupations have been designated as semi-professional rather than as having achieved fully professional status. In our society, women do not share power equally with men. What is particularly ironic is that semi-professionals tend to have control over large areas that deal both with uncertainty and with practices that are difficult to define (indeterminate). Relationships between social workers and clients, school teachers and students, nurses and patients are often focused on issues that require a great deal of professional competence and skill. And yet this frequently goes unrecognized by the general public.

Parents often feel that they can teach better than teachers. I've never met a social worker who hasn't been told by a family member or friend how to do his or her job better, how to deal with a particular problem, or what policy should be adopted to deal with a particular complex of social problems.

Several years back, when I managed a large and, by all standards, successful continuing education program for professionals in the human services, I was faced with some interesting challenges. Psychiatrists, for example, were loathe to register for family treatment courses and workshops offered under the auspice of the School of Social Work, despite the fact that these programs were of an extraordinarily high quality. Psychiatrists, I was told, were just not going to admit their ignorance before people whom they did not consider to be colleagues and who were members of an occupational group of a lower social status.

Interestingly, I found that many social workers seeking management training were willing to pay three or four times the fees charged by the School of Social Work at management workshops conducted by the Business School. Again, I was convinced that the training programs offered under our auspices were equally as good and often better because they were directly aimed at the practice problems faced by managers in human service organizations. In fact, we frequently used the same instructors, after having worked closely with them to help reshape their presentations to deal with issues of importance to social agency managers.

I have to share one anecdote with you. The director of the state department of mental health in a midwestern state, a psychiatrist with very few biases about other occupations, had asked me to develop a course on consultation for directors of community mental health centers. At the time, state law required directors to be psychiatrists. "Thanks for your confidence," I said, "but it'll never work. Psychiatrists are just not going to come to a School of Social Work to learn about consultation." "Oh yes they will," he replied, pulling a set of new forms from his briefcase. "These are the reporting forms that I'm requiring all community mental health center directors to complete before they get reimbursed by the state for any consultation done by their agency staff members. I know you guys (social workers) know more about consultation than we do, but as far as they're concerned (the psychiatrists), social workers know how to fill out forms. If I tell them they have to come to you to learn how to fill out these forms, they'll be there!"

There may be several ways to cope with semi-professional status. One is to get the support of professional elites in the male-dominated professions. The anecdote I shared with you worked for a particular workshop, but it may not work for an entire occupational grouping. Nevertheless, the principle may be worth pursuing. In this case social work was perceived to possess technical competence and skill that another occupational group did not. If social workers, nurses, schoolteachers, and librarians possess some competence that is sufficiently in demand, they may very well be able to negotiate for greater power or control over their own work.

As you are probably aware, practitioners in these semi-professions tend to work in organizations. As such, they are employees and thus subject to all the bureaucratic forms that prevent employees from using discretion and reduce control over their own work. As physicians increasingly become employees in large-scale medical organizations, they too will find themselves in a similar position to that of other employed professionals.

As we noted in Chapter 3, women are less likely to move up in the organizational hierarchy than are men. Management is still heavily male-dominated. Clearly men are overrepresented in the management of social agencies and as principals or administrators in the school system. The women's movement, as it grows in strength, may lead more women into managerial positions. If so, it is likely to have some impact on the status of the female semi-professions.

There may, however, be another way to cope with semi-professional status, and that is to opt out of the competition altogether. Some years ago, Willard Richan and Allan Mendelsohn argued that social work's search for professionalism is bankrupt. Efforts to claim professional status, they postulated, were self-aggrandizing. This may be the reason for what Epstein has termed social work's "disengagement from the poor." The intellectual pretensions of seeking professional status lead to an erosion in activism and an effort to emulate other occupations that offer higher status and better-paying clients.

Further, acceptance of worker status (in contrast with professional status) may lead to gains for clients as much as for members of the occupation. Thus the successful efforts of teachers to unionize has led to similar efforts among social workers, nurses, and librarians. And the collective bargaining objectives of these unions has often focused on the improvement of services to client populations. Even members of the more established professions, like college professors and physicians, have begun to unionize. Thus the distinctions between the professions and the semi-professions may begin to dissolve. Collective action through unionization may do more to right the imbalance in power between occupational groups than any arguments that might be made about technical competence or superior ethics.

DEPROFESSIONALIZATION

Without being explicit about it, we've already examined some of the forces that may lead to a gradual "deprofessionalization" of the professions. They include the revolt of clients, encroachment and competition from other occupational groupings, and unionization related to employee status. We've also discussed another factor—the potential for using paraprofessionals to do things some professionals do, and other things they may not be able to do as well. Michael

Austin has documented the blurring of demarcations between the professionally trained worker (with a BA or MSW degree) and non-professionals or aides who increasingly assume responsibilities formerly allocated only to those with professional training. For example, case-aides often follow up on released mental patients, formerly the role of a social worker. Information referral specialists with no formal training (other than that received on the job) may carry out tasks that were at one time reserved for community organizers. Even social work's development of case management and its claim for exclusive competence in this area is under attack as aspects of referral and follow-up are delegated to less trained (and less expensive) personnel. Although the paraprofessional "movement," as it was called in the mid-1960s and early 1970s, is hardly a movement anymore, it has spawned a wide variety of new occupational classifications that include people with less than BA degrees who perform intake, assessment and follow-up functions that were formerly the exclusive domain of professional social workers.

Today, even clients have challenged the exclusive domain of the professional worker. Self-help groups, at first resisted by many professionals, have now come to be seen as full partners in the healing process. There are, at present, more than 10,000 associations of self-help groups dealing with issues as diverse as weight control and the reduction of family violence. In many cases, social workers have initiated, guided and then launched these groups toward growing independence.

REVIEW AND TENTATIVE CONCLUSIONS

It's time again to review what we have learned thus far. I'll start. You add your own conclusions.

(1) Professionals profess to know better what to do and how to do specific tasks in relation to specific populations and specified problems.
(2) Professionals claim to possess a body of general and systematized knowledge that can be codified and transmitted to others, to be committed to the public good in contrast with private concerns, to have the right to be self-governing and to have jurisdiction over certain problems and certain client populations with regard to which they should have sole authority.

(3) Professionals have their own distinctive cultures and share characteristics commonly identified with a community. These include history and folklore, a common language and a shared sense of destiny or purpose.

(4) Some occupations are more successful than others in laying claim to full professionalism. Social work, together with other "female" occupations, tends to be designated as a semi-profession. This may be less a factor of its knowledge and areas of competence than of the general perceptions of society about that knowledge and competence. It is to a large extent based on sex-stereotyping and on what have come to be perceived as "appropriate" female roles in our society.

YOUR ADDITIONS

(5)

(6)

(7)

(8)

(9)

(10)

NOTES

1. An anti-poverty program in the early and mid-1970s.
2. Hughes's analysis is substantially encapsuled in the following few paragraphs. For a further explication, see Hughes (1963).
3. Curriculum Resources for Adoption and Foster-care Training was a national project conducted in the mid- to late 1970s.

REFERENCES

Austin, Michael J. (1978). *Professionals and paraprofessionals*. New York: Human Sciences Press.
Barber, Bernard. (1963). Some problems in the sociology of the professions. *Daedalus*, Fall.
Bucher, Rue, & Strauss, Anselm. (1961). Professions in process. *American Journal of Sociology*, Fall.
Buffrin, William, & Rituo, Roger. (1984). Work autonomy and the mental health professional. *Administration in Social Work*, Winter.
Epstein, Irwin. (1970). Professionalization, professionalism, and social work radicalism. *Journal of Health and Social Behavior*, January.
Etzioni, Amitai. [Ed.] (1969). *The semi-professions and their organization*. New York: Free Press.
Friedson, Elliott. [Ed.] (1973). *The professions and their prospects*. Beverly Hills, CA: Sage.
Froland, Charles, Pancoast, Diane L., Chapman, Nancy J., & Kimboko, Priscilla J. (1981). *Helping networks in human services*, (esp. Chap. 8). Beverly Hills, CA: Sage.
Goode, William. (1957). Community within a community: The professions. *American Sociological Review*, Spring.
Greenwood, Ernest. (1957). Attributes of a profession. *Social Work*, Spring.
Haug, Marie. (1973). Deprofessionalization: An alternative hypothesis for the future. In Paul Halmos (Ed.), *Professionalization and social change: A sociological review monograph*. Keele, Staffordshire: University of Keele.
Haug, Marie, & Sussman, Marvin. (1969). Professional autonomy and the revolt of the client. *Social Problems*, Spring.
Helfgot, John. (1974). Professional reform organizations and the symbolic representation of the poor. *American Sociological Review*, Fall.
Hughes, Everett C. [Ed.] (1958). *Men and their work*. New York: Free Press.
Hughes, Everett C. (1983). Professions. *Daedalus*, Fall.
Johnson, Terence. (1972). *The professions and power*. London: Macmillan.
Lauffer, Armand. (1970). *Social actionists come to social work*. Ann Arbor, MI: University Microfilms.
Loewenberg, Frank M. (1968). Social workers and indigenous nonprofessionals: Some structural dilemmas. *Social Work*, July.
Richan, Willard C., & Mendelsohn, Allan R. (1973). *Social work: The unloved profession*. New York: New Viewpoints.

Ritzer, George. (1977). *Working: Conflict and change* (2nd ed.). Englewood Cliffs, NJ: Prentice-Hall.

Roth, Julius. (1974). Professionalism: The sociologist's decoy. *Sociology of Work and Occupations,* January.

Toren, Nina. (1972). *Social work: The case of the semiprofession.* Beverly Hills, CA: Sage.

Walsh, J.L., & Elling, R.H. (1968). Professionalization and the poor: Structural effects of professional behavior. *Journal of Health and Social Behavior,* January.

Chapter 5

BECOMING A COLLEAGUE AND ENTERING THE AGENCY'S CULTURE
Perspectives, Cultures, and Conflicts

Betsy, Mike, Cyndi, and Mary Jo are graduate social work students assigned to do their field practicum at the agency. They are in their second semester at school but in their first semester of practicum assignment when we first meet them. Although each was assigned to a different supervisor (Betsy works in the clinical services department under Yolanda's supervision, Cyndi works on family life education under Millicent's guidance, Mike is assigned to the New Americans Project under Sam's direction, and Mary Jo is a community place-ment worker in Harvey's department), the four were encouraged by their school-based faculty adviser to "network" with each other. Schedules permitting, they meet every Tuesday at lunchtime. Early discussions were revealing.

Cyndi: I came here wanting to become the best social worker I can. I feel that this is a really good placement, and I've got a terrific supervisor. But this is such a complicated place to get to know. There's so many things going on and to learn. Sometimes I feel a little lost, but I think they've (the faculty) prepared us pretty well, especially in our practice courses.

Betsy: I feel the same way. After five months of classroom work, this (the agency) really feels like the real world. But there's so much to learn here.

Mary Jo: Yes, but thank goodness for the classroom preparation. I guess I'm lucky that I worked at an agency for a couple of years before coming back to school. It helps me put everything in perspective. I don't mean that I know how to do all my assignments yet, but I've learned enough about practice so that I can talk to Harvey (her supervisor) and the other staff pretty comfortably.

Mike: I don't know. I feel like things that I'm going to be doing are real important, but I feel so inadequate. I'm not used to feeling that way. I guess it's going to take a while, sort of absorbing the atmosphere and learning what's appropriate and what's not. I wanted to work with some Vietnamese families right away, but Sam held me back. Told me to walk around the neighborhood and just observe.

Cyndi: I'm doing some observing too. I agree with Betsy. There's so much to learn.

The conversation then focused on some of the ambiguity that the students were feeling about their roles in the agency. If there was consensus about anything, it was that the agency was a good place to *learn,* that what they were doing or would soon be doing was "real social work," not just classroom theory. That didn't mean denigrating what they were learning in the classroom; if anything, they wanted a chance to see how it could be applied. Two of the students expressed some frustration over having been assigned to different departments. "I know I'm going to have to work hard at it to be a good clinician," Betsy said. "But I'm envious of some of the things you guys are doing. I guess I really want to do everything, learn everything. It's all going to help me when I graduate." "It would have been easier starting out," Mike added, "if we had all been assigned to a single unit at the beginning of our field placements."

* * * * *

The discussion represented a certain diffuseness. Like other students in the early part of their professional training, they wanted to learn everything that would enable them to be good and effective practitioners. They also wanted to apply what they were learning in the classroom, and they were somewhat frustrated at the slowness with which they were assigned responsibilities. "I'm really willing to work hard," Mary Jo had said. "I'd even put in more than the hours that are required if I thought that what I was doing was really being helpful to somebody, and that I was *learning* something from it." "I feel the same way," responded Mike. "But I've got other pressures, too. I've got to watch my time, 'cause I'm working part-time and I don't want my class work to suffer. Getting A's is important to me."

In effect, what was happening was that the students were beginning to define their situation and to establish priorities for themselves. *Learning* clearly was the priority. But they were trying to reconcile what they perceived to be differences between learning in the field and learning in the classroom. The Tuesday lunch conversation two months later, about halfway into their first term in the field, reflected some of the same concerns but was beginning to take a somewhat different turn.

Betsy: I'm still trying to learn everything, but I'm beginning to realize that maybe it's just not possible.

Mary Jo: You can't do it all. Even in my own department where everybody kind of shares the workload, you have to set priorities.

Betsy: The way you and Mike talk about your assignments is so different from mine. Maybe our department is just structured differently. We each (other clinicians) have our own caseloads, and while we sometimes share problems at staff meetings where we case each other's clients, we're each expected to work independently. I get a lot of support from Yolanda. I want to learn all I can from her.

Mike: I feel the same way about Sam. He's got a lot to give, and a lot to teach, stuff that's not in the textbooks and in the coursepacks. I mean, he's really been there, he knows where it's at.

Cyndi: Sometimes I feel my supervisor (Millicent) isn't giving me enough responsibility. But she's really pushing me to get to know myself and how I respond to things. I really want to please her.

*   *   *   *   *

At this point, the students' perspectives seemed to be shifting from the diffuse and long-term ("I want to learn everything I can") to the more realistic and short-term ("I want to please my supervisor" and

"You can't do it all"). They were also beginning to look to the agency more and to the school less for cues about appropriate practice behavior. While they were still finding their support group helpful in confronting their common plight as student interns in a professional agency, they were also beginning to identify themselves more closely with their supervisors and the departments to which they were assigned. Clearly, getting to know everything was taking second place to performing effectively and appropriately as defined by the supervisor and perhaps by others in the department.

About six weeks later, Betsy, Cyndi, and Mike attended a Tuesday brown bag luncheon.

Mike:	Should we wait for Mary Jo?
Betsy:	She's not coming today. She's having lunch with my supervisor and some of the other Black social workers. They have something they call the BiB club—BiB, for "Black is beautiful," I guess (shrugs her shoulders).
Cyndi:	I don't think I can make it next week, either. I mean, there's a lot to do in the family life education program. We've got a big conference coming up. Millicent's expecting a lot from me, and I don't want to disappoint her. I hope you don't mind (raises her eyebrows and wrinkles her nose).

By the middle of the second semester in the field, the students were hardly ever able to make a quorum. "I don't feel so much like a student around here anymore," Cyndi explained to Millicent at one of her weekly supervisory sessions. "I mean, sure, I know I'm a student, but I feel more like a professional worker. Even though I'm here only three days a week (the students were on campus on Thursdays and Fridays), I feel really identified with the agency and especially with the family life education program. I mean, you've given me some real responsibilities, and I feel like I'm part of a team.

"I find myself talking less about school here at the agency, and more about the agency back at school. In fact, the only time Betsy, Mike, Mary Jo, and I ever get together is in our staff development and training class. We talk about the agency a lot. I'm lucky that the assignment I have for that class fits naturally into the kind of things that I'm doing here (at the agency). The others are having a little harder time, but we're each designing programs that we're trying to put into practice here at the center."

* * * * *

DEVELOPING PERSPECTIVE AND ENTERING THE WORK CULTURE

There are a number of concepts through which we might analyze the progression of Cyndi's identity from that of student to that of responsible agency worker and a member of her departmental team. I'm going to use two: "perspective" and "culture." Half a century ago, Karl Mannheim observed that the way in which we conceive things is determined in part by the social or cultural setting in which we find ourselves. George Herbert Mead observed that when people face problematic situations, they attempt to develop coordinated views that guide their actions. He called this the emergence of *perspective*.

In the examples given above, the definition of the problem situation changed for the students over time. Initially the problem was how to cope with the ambiguities and the multiple demands made on them in the agency. Their initial perspectives grew out of collective experiences—the experiences they'd shared at the university, and the experience of being new and unsure at the agency.

Before developing perspectives in common, they relied on those learned elsewhere or borrowed from others. For example, at first they reflected some of the perspectives of their faculty, attempting (or at least hoping) to make a systematic application of classroom knowledge to the work situation. Mary Jo drew in part on her earlier work experiences. Wanting to learn everything at first, they soon limited their aspirations to something more realistic: satisfying one's supervisor and doing one's work well and effectively (limited as that work might be). The changes in perspective were in part the result of facing problems in common with other students, but increasingly they found themselves dealing with work-related problems that they had in common with staff members in the departments to which they were assigned. Eventually, as we shall see, their perspectives became those of colleagues in those work units rather than those of students.

I'm using the term *perspective* much as Howard S. Becker and his associates used it in a study of student culture in the medical school. Drawing on Mead's definition, it refers to a coordinated set of ideas and actions that a person uses in dealing with some problematic situation. It is reflected in a person's ordinary way of thinking and feeling and acting. We all bring different perspectives to our work. Those perspectives are based on earlier experiences and, to a larger extent, on our identification with others whose opinions we value. Robert Merton called this "reference group" behavior. I'm certain you have been in a situation where, in taking action, you asked yourself how someone else whose opinion you respect might respond to what you were doing. In turn, what you were doing and how you were doing it might to a large extent have been influenced by your expectation that this someone might approve or disapprove of certain actions. We all do this as we learn to differentiate between what we perceive to be appropriate and inappropriate in given situations.

This may lead to the emergence of short-term and long-term perspectives. Short-term perspectives include *initial* (I want to learn everything I can), *intermediate* (I want to satisfy my supervisor), and *final* (I want to fit in around here) stages. These may or may not articulate with *long-term* perspectives (I want to be the best social worker I can be).

Although individuals may at first bring different perspectives to bear on a common situation, as they interact with each other they develop group or common perspectives—modes of thought and action that guide their behavior. I'm not talking here about attitudes or values. Values are not necessarily situationally specific. In fact, they tend to be generalized and abstract. They help us evaluate what is good or what is bad, desired or undesired, but not necessarily what is appropriate or inappropriate in a given context. Whereas values may lead to a general predisposition that we may choose to ignore in a given situation, perspectives contain judgments about specific situations and tend to lead to action.

I've always been amazed at how students at the University of Michigan School of Social Work seem to know how long a term paper is supposed to be. I rarely give them guidelines, but by the time they've reached the second semester they know that 10-12 pages will be acceptable, and that somewhere between 15 and 30 footnotes is the norm. How do they learn this if it is never stated explicitly? Attitudes are personal and also provide some predisposition to act in one way or another, but they don't compel us to act. Perspectives do, however, because they are arrived at collectively by those persons involved in interactive situations and who face a common problem. Harvey Marcus reflects on some learning and unlearning he had to do as a teenager and young adult. "People sometimes call me a workaholic," he says with an ingraciating smile, "but I'm not. Sure, I work hard, but I work to get results. My staff expects me to work hard, and I expect them to. And none of us are afraid of putting in some extra time, evenings or weekends, when needed. Look, I'm not a rate buster. I learned long ago that rate busters get punished.

"When I was a kid, working on a kibbutz in Israel, I worked my *butt* off. Everybody did. As a matter of fact, the harder you worked and the more productive you were, the more status and prestige you had. You were, after all, contributing something to the common good, and hard work was really valued. Then when I returned to the States and got a job on the night shift in a factory while working on my undergraduate degree, I learned that not everybody shared those values. At first, I figured if I worked a little harder then I was required to, I could take an extra long break and crack some of the books for my morning classes. I soon learned that rate busters weren't much appreciated. It wasn't what people said to me, it was the fact that they didn't say anything, that they shunned me at breaktime. At first, I didn't catch on. Finally, one person did say that if I worked my part of the line faster than the others, pretty soon everybody'd have to be working at the same rate. The union wasn't going to like it.

"I don't mean to be saying that as a way of patting myself on the back. People develop certain expectations of themselves and of each other. They figure that everybody who's in the same boat ought to be pulling their oars together. I suppose that's correct. Only on some boats, everybody pulls their oars faster than folks on other boats."

The emergence of perspective leads to a body of collective understandings that influence the behavior of people in specific roles. When the perspectives that people hold are related to the positions they occupy in an organization, we can say that an organizational culture is emerging. As a matter of fact, it may result in two cultures: a "management culture" and a "worker culture."

Exercise 5.1

Identifying Perspectives

1. List the perspectives held by the students whose experiences were described here.
    a. Long-Term

    b. Short-Term
       (1) *inital* (on first entering the agency)

       (2) *intermediate* or provisional (toward the middle or end of the first semester)

       (3) *final* (end of second semester in the field)

2. Which of these perspectives would you define as realistic/ unrealistic? Why?

3. Do you think their perspectives complement or conflict with those of their field instructors (supervisor) and of the faculty at the School of Social Work? If so, how? If not, why?

4. Now describe a situation in which your perspective changed over time. How did those changes occur?

Agency culture or cultures take on characteristics of their own. The culture informs people subtly about the rights and privileges they possess and the duties and obligations associated with particular positions. While the culture may be influenced by the work situation, it also tends to be influenced by external factors: the norms, values, and ethics inherent in the profession to which the majority or dominant staff members belong, and the larger societal culture. In fact, the various subcultures in the larger society may have considerable influence on agency practice and on the perspectives of agency staff members.

Sometimes these cultures clash. Thus, as we saw in Chapter 4, Sam's efforts to develop a cadre of paraprofessionals who are more reflective of the cultures of the New Americans for whom he has responsibility came into conflict with the professional culture that dominates the agency staff's perspectives.

CULTURE SHOCK

"Just before my last semester in school," Betsy recalled, two years after we first met her, "I told Yolanda that I wanted a community organization experience. There wasn't much chance for me to do any kind of outside work in the clinical services department. Yolanda agreed with me that working with Harvey Marcus in the community placement department might give me just the kind of opportunity I was looking for. But she warned me about the 'culture shock' I'd be likely to face. And was she on target!

"It really was like going from one culture to another. In clinical services, we did extensive diagnosis and testing and we provided clinical counseling. It may be true that we (the staff in the department) didn't all use exactly the same approaches to counseling—about half the staff were behaviorists, and the others were analytic in their approaches—but we had a more or less formal organization and everybody did their job in pretty much the same way. What I mean is, it was like a 9 to 5 place. We saw clients, you know, the 50-minute hour bit, and we recorded our notes, and we 'staffed' difficult cases together when necessary. It was all very professional.

"Sure, we did some follow-up and sometimes it was necessary to do home visits or to meet with professionals in some other organizations on behalf of the client—you know, like schools, the courts, the nursing home—and the standards were high. I mean, it's a good department. Very professional. You would expect that with somebody like Yolanda as a supervisor. I mean, people dress for the job. I wouldn't have thought of wearing my student clothes at the agency.

"Now, the community placement department, it was like a different world. A lot of the men wore jeans, and the women wore slacks. I don't think I ever saw Harvey wearing a tie except when he had to go to the state capitol or when he was off to some foundation hunting up a grant. Nobody ever closed their office doors, and there was a lot of working together. Maybe it's because we didn't see so many clients individually. Most of our clients, if we had any, were out in the community, in placement or needing placement. Mostly we worked on finding and licensing group homes, and then supervising or consulting with them. And, of course, a lot of people working in the group homes dress pretty informally.

"I mean, they would have to. You aren't going to be dressed up in a suit if you're working with staff who supervise kids in a group foster home, or with people who run adult group foster homes for senior citizens and ex-mental patients. I guess you could say the way we dressed at the agency was the way in which our clients—the providers of direct services to people needing placement—dressed. Maybe that's the way they expected us to dress. But dress wasn't the only thing.

"It was the way staff were always throwing out and testing new ideas. It wasn't just Harvey's style, although he encouraged it. But it was like, if there was a better way to do it, we should be trying it. No rigid behavioral or Freudian approaches here. I don't mean to say that people were rigid in the clinical services program, but they were tight. Here, everybody hung loose. It didn't matter what theory you used. Any idea, if it worked, was good.

"At first, I was really upset. It wasn't just because I had to move out of the office and into the community, either locating neighborhoods where we could put in a group home, or organizing community groups to support the work of some of those homes. That's what I was looking for, a CO assignment. And I knew that community workers tended to be more informal than some others in the profession. But I really found the style shocking. Maybe it's me, and my own rigid way of looking at things. But I don't think so. It just didn't seem to me that these people were professional, if you know what I mean.

"I don't know, but I think I'd have a hard time going back to Yolanda's department. I've come to respect and appreciate the openness and the give and take of the community placement staff. They're not any less serious, or any less professional than anybody else that I've worked with. Maybe they're more so. They really work hard at what they do. And they're committed. I mean, they really care, and not just from 9 to 5. They're doing real advocacy work. And that's real social work."

* * * * *

Like professions and other occupations, all organizations develop their own cultures, complete with taboos, folkways and mores. Within limits, it is possible for a single organization to develop a number of subcultures, so long as they reflect the general norms and values of the larger system. These cultures reflect the history of the department or the organization, its internal structure and the way in which it deals with its external relationships. It may be influenced by the types of people the organization attracts, its work processes, physical layouts, modes of communication, and the exercise of authority within the system. The culture in turn exerts its own influence.

The organization or the units within it will develop collective feelings and beliefs about the appropriate way to do things and pass these on to group members. Perspectives developed in the past are imposed on those who enter the organization or the unit within it. Thus the culture of each organizational unit provides a frame of reference within which members interpret the appropriateness of certain activities and actions.

Interestingly, while members may be clear about why they do things, they are not likely to be aware of the basic frames of reference that they use in arriving at certain judgments. The differences between one unit and another only become clear when someone like Betsy crosses from one environment into the other. As Betsy pointed out, the nature of the interaction in relationships with the unit's clients may have something to do with the emergence of a certain culture within the unit. This may become even clearer if we examine client

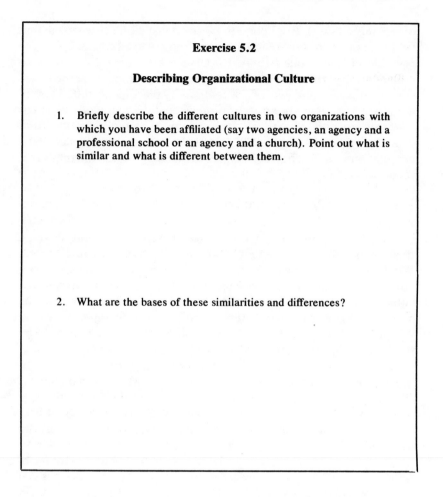

Exercise 5.2

Describing Organizational Culture

1. Briefly describe the different cultures in two organizations with which you have been affiliated (say two agencies, an agency and a professional school or an agency and a church). Point out what is similar and what is different between them.

2. What are the bases of these similarities and differences?

influences on the New Americans Project. Recall the discussion in the previous chapter.

* * * * *

Here it was two days after the staff meeting where Sam Mansouri's proposal for a paraprofessional program had been shot down, and Sam was still wondering what had happened and why. At least Harvey should have supported the proposal. After all, Harvey was a friend. They had known each other in graduate school, and while Sam had been in the clinical track while Harvey was a community organization student, they had taken a number of classes together and were immediately drawn to each other.

The fact that one was an Arab from Lebanon and the other an American Jew who had spent time in Israel is what initially attracted them. As Sam explains it: "Because my family are Maronite Christians, we always felt somewhat marginal in the Middle East. When I was younger, I listened to Israeli music on the radio a lot and watched Israeli programs on television. I dreamt for peace between our peoples. When I met Harvey, I found someone who was an American Jew and who also understood marginality. But he had also shared some Middle Eastern experiences and yearned like I did for peace between our peoples."

Because Harvey was an American, and born in this country, Sam marveled at the ease with which Harvey moved into leadership positions, often taking on liberal political causes, and often challenging conventional wisdom. This is what particularly perplexed him about Harvey's lack of support at the meeting. He decided to drop in on Harvey that afternoon to find out what was going on. Was it him (Sam)? Was it the way he had made the presentation? Was it something in the agency's climate that he had missed?

"Look, old buddy," Harvey explained later that afternoon. "For a guy who's really sensitive to culture and cultural differences, you really missed the boat on this one. My staff and I can get away with all kinds of things that you can't. We're kind of on the periphery of the agency. We don't work directly with individual clients. We work with community groups and other agencies. So because the case worker and educator types on the staff don't quite understand what we do, they don't impose the same standards on our practice as they impose on yours.

"But you're providing direct services to people, and this agency thinks of itself as a direct service agency, and it has high professional standards. You've got three things working against you. First, you're dealing with populations that the rest of the agency staff are not competent to deal with, or at least we know that their methods won't work. Your clients are not Westerners, and the way in which they handle problems is not the way in which we're equipped to help them. So you're already putting demands on us with the New Americans

Project that not only require sensitivity to the cultures of Asian and Arab populations, but that may challenge our cherished ways of helping people deal with problems.

"Second, there's a high premium put here (at the agency) on professional standards. It's only natural that people will be afraid that we might dilute those standards by including less than professionally trained people on the staff. I don't think people are worrying about their jobs, but they are worrying that they, *we,* won't be doing our jobs to quite the standards we value. You were saying to us that our methods don't work, and that some other people with less training will be more effective. Well, that's a pretty strong challenge, and we weren't ready to deal with it.

"But the biggest problem is that you violated some pretty important norms around here about the way in which we make decisions. Look, you've been around long enough to know that this is a pretty open agency. We really do make decisions collectively. But we never make them formally until we've already made them informally. You brought in a whole new proposal without properly preparing us. People just weren't ready to deal with your recommendations. You didn't give those ideas a chance to percolate, to kind of bubble up over time. I mean, Yolanda and certainly Millicent would have been more open if they'd had a chance to think about the issues more and had been able to develop a professional rationale for what you were suggesting. You just don't bring new ideas to a staff meeting. We rarely don't make tough decisions at staff meetings. Can you remember a single incident in which there was as much feeling and anger expressed about a new proposal? I can't. And it had nothing to do with your proposal. It had to do with the fact that we weren't ready for it.

"You may be feeling bad about the way things went, and you've got the biggest stake in it. But they're feeling pretty bad, too. First of all, no one likes to turn down a colleague. But they're also feeling violated because you sprung one on them that they weren't ready for."

* * * * *

Harvey left something out of his analysis. What he was unaware of, because he himself had only been at the agency six years, was that in the early 1970s the All-Families Service Center had built up a fairly extensive paraprofessionals' program as part of its efforts to extend services to a low-income housing complex. While initially the program had met with some success, it had backfired when the paraprofessionals had begun to advocate for clients against the agency itself, defining the agency as the tool of the "white racist establishment." The aftermath had left its residue of bitterness. Even the term "paraprofessional" had become a red flag, *red* in more than one sense. History has a way of influencing norms, attitudes, values, and perspectives. As they become ingrained into agency culture, they are likely to endure over time, even when circumstances change.

HOW MIGHT SAM HAVE BETTER PREPARED THE STAFF?

Sam might have been more successful if he had begun by sensitizing other staff members to both the special needs and special characteristics of the "New American" populations that his department was serving. This he might have done by participating in case conferences conducted within the clinical services department whenever issues pertaining to the agency's Southeast Asian or Chaldean clients came up.

In doing so, he would have had an opportunity to point out that establishing a working relationship with clients from a particular background depends at least in part on having genuine respect for that background. And such respect requires an understanding of the client's culture. He might also have sought opportunities to work collaboratively with the family life education program that Millicent directs. One cannot expect new Americans to function as old Americans. They bring with them to their new country established concepts of sharing, of familial relationships, of acceptance of suffering, of optimism, and of self-help that are indigenous to their own cultures.

For some cultures, social work techniques of communication that focus on the individual client may not be appropriate. The social and familial networks through which new Americans seek help must be understood. For people coming from traditional cultures, the help-seeking pattern usually includes going for help to family members first, and that family may include an extended family kinship network—aunts and uncles, cousins, and others from the same village. It may also include seeking help from a religious leader. Only when these networks are incapable of helping will new Americans consider seeking help from institutional providers.

Moreover, help from institutions like the All-Families Service Center is not likely to be productive (whether it is focused on intrapsychic problems, housing, job seeking, and so on) unless such help takes into account the availability of supports in the external network. And those supports are likely to be present only if members of the network perceive them as being appropriate—that is, contributing to the maintenance of the network and in keeping with long-standing values and traditions.

Americanization need not include de-Vietnamization or de-Arabization. However, it does require helping new Americans make use of all their internal resources in connecting with and making use of new resources in the American environment. This may require changes in technique and even in personnel, but it need not require changes in social work's basic value orientations.

Gisella Knopka and others have made this point quite clear. Social work practices are based on two absolute values: a respect for the dignity of the individual, and a commitment to encouraging the responsibility of individuals and communities for the less fortunate. But these values can be applied differently. Americans prize individuality, while other cultures may prize the family and the group culture more highly. In traditional cultures, even significant personal aspirations may be understood best within the context of the larger group from which the individual comes.

Thus responsibility for others in some cultures belongs to the family and the immediate members of a network. Institutions like social agencies may be perceived as distant and foreign, and social work and educational interventions that ignore such cultural patterns are not likely to be successful. Certainly Millicent is aware of this. Her practice experiences in South America were built directly on people's own experiences and their interpretation of their situations. Yolanda's sensitivity to her own cultural heritage includes a deep awareness of what it means to be left out, to be misunderstood and to be defined as deviant or alien.

With these facts in mind, it might have been possible for Sam to bring others to the conclusion that the agency would be more effective if it involved representatives of the two cultures as outreach workers and as case-aides. Further, by using the terminology "outreach worker" and "case-aide" he would have avoided raising the red flag of paraprofessionalism.

If you have suggested approaches that increase the likelihood that decisions and actions will be taken in a collegial manner, you are on the right track. Colleagues are associates, fellows in the same organization or profession. Colleagues, you will recall, must be able to take each other's sentiments for granted. They must be able to communicate freely and openly among themselves and to share confidences that will not be repeated to uninitiated ears. If Sam can't share with others his professional concerns about the populations for whom he's responsible because he's overly defensive of them or because he doesn't feel that the staff will understand or appreciate the uniqueness of their cultures, then he is not fully accepting the other staff members as colleagues.

One's professional colleagues are defined as those who have similar training, similar values and who are engaged in similar core tasks. That may be why the students we looked in on earlier in this chapter felt a collegial bond to each other at the beginning of their work at the agency but soon found themselves pulling apart as they developed stronger collegial relationships to people in the particular units to which they were assigned.

While one might feel closest to those engaged in a similar practice, one also feels close to those performing similar roles in a different department in an agency. Thus supervisors might find much in common with each other and less in common with supervisees doing the same kind of work that the supervisor may have performed only a few months earlier. To a large extent, these changes occur because people perceive themselves as being "in the same boat." You'll recognize in this discussion much of what we said earlier about reference group behavior, and about the development of common perspectives.

DEALING WITH CONFLICTS IN THE AGENCY

Throughout these chapters, we've dealt with a number of sources of conflict within the organization. Conflict can be instrumental or expressive; or it can be ideological or operational. I'll explain.

The conflict that erupted briefly between Yolanda and some of her white colleagues was an example of *expressive* conflict (see Chapter 2). It was the result of the accumulation of tension and a need to

---

Exercise 5.3

Innovating on the Basis of Cultural Differences

Considering what you now know about Sam et al., the other workers in the agency and the initial responses to Sam's proposal, how
would you advise him? What should he do next?

---

release hostile feelings. It may have also been the result of error and
ignorance on her part, and on the part of others. Sam's response to
"defeat" at the meeting of the agency's supervisory staff was also
perceived by him in expressive terms. It was perceived by others,
however, both expressively and instrumentally. *Instrumental* conflict
tends to be marked by opposing practices or goals.

Instrumental conflict may be further perceived as either ideological or operational in nature. When it is defined as a conflict in basic
values, it becomes ideological, and decisions are made (the conflict is
resolved or one side wins) on the basis of what people perceive to be
"right" or "wrong." When the conflict, however, is perceived to be
operational in nature, it may be resolved on the basis of perceptions of
effectiveness and ineffectiveness. Sam was defining a problem operationally, while others were perceiving it both operationally and
ideologically.

Conflict may also be defined as inherent or induced. *Inherent* conflicts arise from irreconcilable differences in a given situation. For example, while the conflict was not perceived as intense, there was clearly a conflict between Betsy, Cyndi, Mike, and Mary Jo's identity as students and their identification with their supervisors and work units. It was resolved by reducing student identity and increasing departmental identity. Conflicts can also be *induced* artificially for strategic purposes.

Induced conflict is purposive. Differences may be highlighted so as to promote recognition of alternatives which might otherwise remain hidden from view. It might also be used to increase coherence within a particular group. Could Sam have used conflict more purposefully, or more strategically?

The presence or absence of conflict will vary from agency to agency and from time to time. Around any given issue, there may be a great deal of conflict or virtually none. For example, when everyone agrees that a procedure is correct or that a particular population deserves expanded services, one might find consensus on both means and goals. By definition, such consensus would reflect an absence of conflict. In such circumstances, an appropriate strategy would be to bring the consenting parties together for purposes of developing a plan of action.

There may, however, be considerable difference of opinion, perhaps even indifference to the issues at hand. Under such circumstances it wouldn't do to bring the interested parties together, because they are basically disinterested. But highlighting the issue, developing a critical consciousness of it, may lead to interest and commitment. Much of Millicent's work as an adult educator is aimed at generating just such interest and commitment.

When there is clear disagreement on goals or procedures, conflicts of interest may be present. If these are intense, it may do no good to ignore them. It may be more appropriate to line up support on one side in order to attempt to beat the opposition. In some agencies this may be possible. However, in the All-Families Service Center, using a contest strategy of this sort would clearly be a violation of agency norms. Sam could not have won any battle perceived of as conflictive in nature. The collegial nature of decision making could not accommodate it. Conflict, if it was to be reconciled, had to be dealt with indirectly and resolved informally. The collective stake of the staff in preserving a climate of cooperation, collegiality and professionalism did not permit any other means of resolving conflict. In other agencies, a different set of mechanisms might exist. These could include arbitration or decision making by those in higher levels of authority, structured and open debates on differences of opinion regarding appropriate practices or value stances or the creation of third-party interventions to mediate conflicts (for example, appeal procedures). I don't mean to imply by this discussion that conflict is unnatural to an organization. To the contrary. Conflict is normal to all social institutions. Without conflicts of interest and perspectives, one would hardly expect organizations to change, grow or develop. Conflict is only destructive if there are no ways to handle it, and if it leads to disintegration rather than integration. By integration, I mean the way in which elements in a social organization become connected so as to give unity to the total organization.

The All-Families Service Center is clearly characterized by a great deal of diversity in its services, yet it maintains a considerable degree of integration in its sense of mission and professionalism. The diversity in programs and services, in fact, may be an instrument of such integration, permitting staff to pursue a wide variety of intervention approaches, and thus minimizing the conflict that might arise if they had to argue out the benefits of one approach or another within a single staff grouping. It is only when the practices in a particular unit seem to contradict or conflict with the practices of another (as in Sam's example) that conflict surfaces and becomes intrusive.

REVIEW AND TENTATIVE CONCLUSIONS

Let's review what we've added to our understanding of work in an organizational setting.

(1) When people work together or face problems in common over time, they develop a common or collective perspective on what to do and how to act. This perspective may be mediated by earlier experiences and role models, but it is nevertheless strongly influenced by the current situation.

(2) Perspectives can be long- or short-term. The latter go through initial, intermediate and final (relatively permanent) stages.

Exercise 5.4

Identifying Conflict Situations

1. You have undoubtedly experienced a variety of conflict situations in your own professional work experiences. Thinking back on these experiences or drawing from illustrations in the text, sketch out examples of:

Instrumental Conflicts	Expressive Conflicts
Inherent Conflicts	Induced Conflicts
Ideological Conflicts	Operational Conflicts

2. How frequently do these conflicts occur? How intense are they? How long do they last?
    Rate each of the conflict situations you have described.
    —VF (very frequent), F (frequent), NF (not frequent)
    —VI (very intense), I (intense), NI (not intense)
    —VL (very long), L (long), NL (not long)

3. To resolve any one of these conflicts, how might things be redefined (e.g., from expressive to instrumental, from ideological to operational or from expressive to ideological, etc.)?
    Describe, and explain your reasons.

(3) Perspectives are related to the emergence of a group or organizational culture. Such culture is shaped by a common history as well as by external environmental or societal forces. The culture finds expression in norms, values, folkways, decision-making processes, dress, and other behaviors. While agencies have overall cultures, alternative expressions of such cultures, and sometimes even different cultures, may be found in different departments. Moving from one department or organization to another may entail a certain amount of culture shock when accustomed patterns are challenged by other ways of viewing and doing things.

(4) Agencies are not conflict-free. Conflicts may take on expressive or instrumental forms. Expressive conflict is often the result of accumulated tension, whereas instrumental conflict relates more to differences in ideological or operational approaches to practice. Some conflicts are inherent, built into a situation, whereas others are induced and then purposefully brought into the open so that issues can be dealt with.

YOUR ADDITIONS

(5)

(6)

(7)

(8)

(9)

(10)

REFERENCES

Ayers, Robert, & Nachamkin, Beverly. (1982). Sex and ethnic differences in the use of power. *Journal of Applied Psychology, 67*(4).

Becker, Howard S., Geer, Blanche, Hughes, Everett C., & Strauss, Anselm. (1976). *Boys in white: Student culture in medical school.* Chicago: University of Chicago Press.

Cohen, Lynn R. (1982). Minimizing communicative breakdowns between male and female managers. *Personnel Administrator,* October.

Coser, Louis A. (1957). Social conflict and the theory of social change. *British Journal of Sociology,* September.

Dahrendorf, Ralf. (1958). Towards a theory of social conflict. *Journal of Conflict Resolution,* Spring.

Delgado, Melvin. (1979). Hispanic staff in non-Hispanic settings: Issues and recommendations. *Administration in Social Work, 3*(4), Winter.

Gudykunst, William, Stewart, Leon P., & Ting-Toomey, Stella. (1985). *Communication, culture and organizational processes.* Beverly Hills, CA: Sage.

Hughes, Everett C. (1958). License and mandate. In E. C. Hughes (Ed.), *Men and their work.* New York: Free Press.

Jayaratne, Srinika, & Chess, Wayne A. (1984). The effects of emotional support on perceived job stress and strain. *Journal of Applied Behavioral Science,* March.

Knopka, Gisella. (1971). Cultural differences in social work philosophy. *International Social Work,* January.

Lewis, M. (1980). Surprise and sense-making: What newcomers experience in entering unfamiliar organizational settings. *Administrative Science Quarterly, 25*(2), June.

Mannheim, Karl (1936). *Ideology and utopia.* London: Routledge & Kegan Paul.

Martin, Joanne, Feldman, Marthe, Hatch, Mary Jo, & Sitkin, Sim B. (1983). The uniqueness paradox in organizational stories. *Administrative Science Quarterly,* September.

Mead, George Herbert. (1938). *The philosophy of the act.* Chicago: University of Chicago Press, 1938.

Merton, Robert. (1957). *Social theory and social structure.* New York: Free Press.

Olsen, Marvin E. (1978). *The process of social organization.* New York: Holt, Rinehart & Winston.

Pernell, Ruby B. (1970). Social work values on the new frontiers. In Katherine A. Kendall (Ed.), *Social work values in an age of discontent.* New York: Council on Social Work Education.

Smirchick, Linda. (1983). Concepts of culture in organizational analysis. *Administrative Science Quarterly,* September.

Specht, Harry. (1972). The deprofessionalization of social work. *Social Work,* February.

Suk, Gerald. (1966). The go-between process in family therapy. *Family Process,* April.

Thompson, James D. (1960). Organizational management in conflict. *Administrative Science Quarterly,* March.

Tjosvold, Dean. (1984). Making conflict productive. *Personnel Administrator,* June.

Van Wagner, Karen, & Swanson, Cheryl. (1977). From Machiavelli to Ms.: Differences in male-female power styles. *Public Administration Review,* February.

Wallach, Ellen J. (1983). Individuals and organizations: The cultural match. *Training and Development,* February.

Walter, Richard. (1969). *Interpersonal peacemaking.* Reading, MA: Addison-Wesley.

Chapter 6

GETTING THE JOB DONE AND
GETTING ALONG
Tasks, Roles, and Responsibilities at Work

Carl Farrell was more than a little apprehensive when Bill Clapman, the Center's director, asked him to drop by for a chat. Things had not been going well for Carl. When he'd first come to the agency ten years earlier to take over the accounting department, Carl had been in his mid-30s, at the peak of his professional competence. Within a few years he'd helped the agency restructure its rather chaotic fiscal practices. Those had been exhilirating years.

In those days the agency was still in its growth phase, and Carl knew that the procedures he'd developed had given management greater control over its programs. Control was one of those things that Carl liked. There was something about taking a jumble of figures, even a mess of figures, and organizing them, that gave him a deep sense of satisfaction. It also felt good to get positive feedback from others at the agency. The others weren't like Carl; they were people-oriented. "I'm a numbers man," he often thought to himself, "but I really appreciate the kinds of things they (the social work staff) do." Nevertheless, over the years things had gone progressively sour for Carl. "Maybe it's the work, maybe it's me," he thought. Work had become routine. There wasn't much challenge to it. And Carl was feeling increasingly isolated. He'd never really shared much or had much in common with the other staff members. "Well, I'm an accountant and they're social workers," he reasoned. But there was something more to it than that.

"Midlife crisis," he'd reasoned. He had felt it coming on for some time. Perhaps that's why he'd gone back to playing the bass a couple of nights a week at Renfrew's. Jazz was Carl's one real outlet. It provided him the structure through which he could be really free, at least for the few hours each night that he played. "Improvisation without commitment," that's how he saw it, an opportunity to let loose. And an opportunity to really relate to other people. "It's like a sexual thing," he confided to his wife. "When we're playing off each other, it's really an act of love. We're saying things that we could never say in words. But then when I leave it, when the gig is over, I really can leave it behind. It's no commitment. I can pack up my fiddle and never look back. It's a real love affair while you're playing, but with no commitments. No strings. When the set's over, it's over."

But work wasn't like that at all. It was more like writing a score that sort of played itself. And there was no intensity in the relationships with the other players. That's the way Carl had wanted it, or so he thought. But it wasn't satisfying. He knew something was missing in his work, and he was certain that Bill saw it too. That's why he wasn't looking forward to what he thought might be coming as he walked into Bill's office.

FROM MANAGING FINANCIAL ASSETS TO MANAGING PEOPLE AS ASSETS

"Carl," Bill began, "over the years, you've helped us all learn to manage our assets more effectively. Now I've got another challenge for you. Tell me what you think." Bill then went through a litany of issues he felt needed to be addressed. "I realized something was wrong," he explained, "when the staff reacted the way it did to Sam's proposal. There's no reason we should not explore alternative staff arrangements for the New Americans Project. Clearly, we've got all kinds of staffing arrangements operating already. Maybe too many. Maybe not enough. Maybe some of our people are trying to defend their own turf or their own ways of operating, I don't know. What I do know is that we've got to get a handle on what's going on. We can be more efficient, and we've got to be more accountable. I think what we need is a job analysis.

"Here, look at this stuff," he continued, handing Carl a number of notebooks. "Take a look here, at this 'task bank' developed by a guy by the name of Sydney Fine at the Upjohn Institute. Mary Jo, one of our students, brought this in. It's a system for identifying every task that's performed in an agency like ours and then rewriting the tasks to the specifications of the job. You then reorder the tasks, as I understand it, and reassign them in some more functional way. I don't understand it all, but I think you should take a look at it. Then I'd like you to pull together a little task force—some key staff people who can help you put together a task bank for our agency. What I'm looking for is some way of rationalizing, of making more systematic the way we assign tasks to different people and to different departments. It's not so different from managing financial assets; it's managing people assets."

Carl was slow to respond at first. "I'm not sure I know enough about what people are doing around here." "That's the point," Bill responded. "I'm not sure any of us really do. But I have a feeling that if we could specify the tasks that have to be performed, we might be a little less defensive about who should perform them." Carl thought about it a bit longer. "I like the idea," he began slowly. "It's a challenge. I'm really not sure I'm the right person for it, but I need a challenge right now. Let's talk about who should be involved. I think Yolanda, Sam for sure, Millicent and Harvey—he's always full of ideas." "And Ali," Bill suggested. "She seems to be trusted by everyone, and it would give her a little more stature around here. Besides, she knows what the clerical staff do. And why not add Mary Jo? It would be a good assignment for her. We should involve our students more."

"I'll give it a try," agreed Carl. "But before I do, I'll want to talk to each of these people to make sure that they really want to participate. I'm not too good at this interpersonal stuff, and I need to feel secure, to be sure, I guess, that they'll want to work with me." "Good," Bill responded. "I'll call them and tell them I asked you to chair a task group to do some exploring into ways in which we might make better use of our staff. I'll explain that I think you're the right person, because you've got a good systematic mind and because you've no stake in any particular department's operations. That should give you the legitimacy you need. Come back and tell me how you decide to proceed after you've had a chance to talk to them all." "Well," thought Carl as he returned to his office, "if I'm going to help write this score, the first thing I better find out is just what the score is." He gave his boss a few days to contact the others and then called Mary Jo.

TASK ANALYSIS: FINDING OUT WHO'S DOING WHAT

Mary Jo explained what she knew about task analysis to Carl. "I think it's real exciting. I worked on a similar process in a job I had before returning to school. I learned more about it in a class on personnel practices, and it gave me a chance to rethink the work I had done at the agency where I worked before. We organized a small team and interviewed everybody at the agency. We used a standard form and got everybody to spell out, as precisely as they could, the tasks that they performed. We tried to group these tasks into 'people' tasks, 'materials' tasks, and 'ideas' tasks. What I mean is that some tasks were almost exclusively related to working with people, like interviewing, counseling, and advising. Other tasks were related to materials, such as filing and typing. Still other tasks were related primarily to ideas—for example, diagnosing, assessing, and evaluating.

"What I mean by *task* is the smallest unit of work that can be described. And to describe a task, you have to build it around an action verb, like some of those that I mentioned: 'counsels,' 'files,' 'records,' 'refers' and 'distributes.' But you need more than just an action verb. You also need a sentence that you build around it.

"A sentence includes the following components: (1) who, (2) performs what action, (3) to whom or to what, (4) using what tools or methods, (5) to what end or for what purpose and (6) using what directions or under whose instructions. For example, you could say, 'The adoption worker writes letters to adoptive parents confirming agency decisions to place a child in their home and informing them of the necessary procedures in order to provide them with the information needed to begin the adoption process, under the direction of the adoption supervisor.'

"Whenever I forget the order in which a sentence should be written, I just think of an example I learned. It works like this: ' (1) The butler (2) laces (3) Mrs. Scarlett's tea (4) with arsenic (5) in order to do her in (6) at the behest of the upstairs maid.'

"One of the nice things about getting everybody to identify the tasks they perform is that you quickly learn that what they are actually doing may be different from what it says in their job descriptions. Not only that, but some people may be performing tasks that they really hate, or that they're not very good at. By finding that out, you can help people share tasks, or shift responsibilities for tasks from one person to the other. That way, people who are better at certain things or who like to do them might take on more responsibility for certain tasks than for others. It's also possible to specify the level at which the tasks should be performed. For example, you could develop criteria for determining whether the letters that the adoption worker writes are clear, warm and empathic in style and contain all the pertinent information. That way you can train people to perform tasks more effectively, correct them if they're making mistakes and use those criteria in supervision.

"But it's not so easy to do, sometimes. Some people are pretty defensive about the tasks they perform and are not so willing to give them up or to let anybody else know what they are doing. I mean, it's like if anybody else knew exactly what they were doing, they would have some of their strength or their power stripped away. And if somebody else decides to reassign tasks from one person to another, there might be some resistance on the part of the people who were getting new assignments and those who were having old and cherished assignments taken away. Know what I mean?"

Carl looked over the forms and procedural manuals that Mary Jo shared with him. He was comfortable with the technical aspects of task analysis. It fit his sense that everything should be kept neat and accountable. "That's what accountants like, after all," he smiled to himself. But he was troubled with what he perceived to be some political aspects of this whole process that could mean potential conflict among staff members. Putting things neatly down on paper, fitting them in appropriate boxes, and showing the relationships between them—these were things Carl felt both at ease with and competent in doing. Dealing with interpersonal relationships, especially if conflict was involved—that's not something he felt comfortable with.

"The best way to handle things is to be straightforward," he thought. "I'll just approach each of the members of the task force, tell them what I've learned from Mary Jo and discuss the charge I got from Bill Clapman. And then I'll ask them what they think."

* * * * *

Millicent's reaction: "Interesting idea. Intriguing. You know, I think I can use this approach in our department's work in training agency volunteers. People come in with all kinds of skills and all kinds of backgrounds. And we've had no way of assessing what they can do and what they can't do. If we could clarify the tasks that we expect them to perform, we could train them for those tasks more adequately, maybe even help them develop their own standards for effective performance. If people know what's expected of them, and where they are in terms of being able to meet those expectations or what they are, they're more likely to be motivated to improve.

"As to using it with the agency's professional staff, I'm not sure. I think about my own work. It's not something I can easily define. No, that's not altogether correct. I suppose I could lay out all the major tasks that I perform. But, you know, my work isn't routine. I'm often involved with the public, particularly when I doing community education or family life education. And often I find myself responding to other people's expectations or their definitions of the problems that they're presenting. What I mean is that other people are likely to shape my work as much as I do myself.

"It's not that I'm not responsible for my work but that my responsibility is to be responsive to others. No, as I think about it, there really are too many external demands and expectations for me to be able to spell out all the tasks that I perform. And I suspect the same would be true with many of the other professional staff members at the agency. Certainly I'm willing to sit down with the rest of the task force to discuss these issues. But I'm not sure it would work, or how. What I am concerned about is any potential limitation on our autonomy and flexibility."

* * * * *

Yolanda responds: "Carl, you've got to be kidding! I can't imagine what Bill has in mind. Sure, it might work for our secretaries, although the routines around here are so clear that I'm not sure that it's worth the effort. But for the caseworkers and other clinicians? No way. "There's something that happens in the relationship between client and worker that you just can't define in neat little boxes. Oh, maybe they can teach clinical practice at the university, but when students get here it's a different world. It's not so much the tasks that we perform, the things that we do, as the way we do them. I guess it's the difference between task and 'technique.' And I don't mean by that anything mechanical. I mean something artistic. What good would it do you to describe the kinds of tasks that Picasso performs? Or what Coleman Hawkins does? Would it yield better understanding? Could you supervise or train people to become a Picasso or a Hawkins?

"You know, clinical practice can be pretty intense. And sometimes there's no way of predicting at the beginning of a session exactly what kinds of things a therapist will do. The more disturbed the client or the more difficult his or her circumstances, and the more emotion involved, the more creative we have to be. We (therapists) are likely to have to draw on a wide variety of skills.

"I mean, we listen, we attend, we mediate, we diffuse, we probe, we redirect, we calm and we energize. Those are all action verbs, like you've been describing for task analysis. But I'm not sure we could ever get a complete inventory. Even if we did, I'm not sure we could properly use them either for allocating responsibilities, for training or for supervising. What really happens in a treatment session, the real stuff of practice, just can't be described with these verbs alone. There's something very personal, almost a magic dynamic that makes true therapeutic communication work. You just can't put that down in a simple sentence."

*   *   *   *   *

Sam responds: "I like it. I really do. This is maybe just the thing that we need to clarify the distinctions between the work of professional staff, volunteers, clericals and paraprofessionals. It's not that we don't know who is who, but we may not know what is what. A lot of us perform similar tasks. Some may even be identical. But the expectations we have of ourselves, in different professional roles, may be quite different. The performance standards we impose on some staff may be at a higher or lower level than we would impose on other staff.

"When I think of my job description, what it really does is it spells out what my official role is at the agency. And it's the same for other staff members. But sometimes we have different expectations of each other in our role performance. This would help clarify what the appropriate expectations might be. And I can see where it could even lead to some negotiations within a department or across departments for the allocation of specific tasks or responsibilities. Maybe even some reshuffling that would lead to greater efficiency and effectiveness. But most important, it would spell out the differences in roles or the jobs that we expect different levels of staff to perform. Yeah, I really do like it.

"You know, as I think about it, while it may not always be so important for clinicians to clarify their own tasks, it is important for them to spell out those tasks for other people with whom we interact. You know, clients don't come here directly. They go through an intake and an assessment process first. Sometimes they are referred by other agencies. After we see them, we may send them to rehabilitation, to the child guidance clinic, to a housing worker, and to a variety of other people who perform a lot of other kinds of tasks. In effect, while we provide them with intensive treatment within our own program, we are really part of a processing chain. That is, the client gets processed at a number of different stations, either here, within the agency, or outside. And sometimes the tasks that are performed by different workers are contradictory with the tasks that are performed by other workers, or else they are duplicative. Sometimes, of course, and if we're lucky, they complement each other.

"But we have no way of really knowing that. Recently, we've begun to do more in the area of case management. And the case managers are the people who could really benefit by some clarity about the tasks that are performed for the client at different stations. Yes, I do think that we could benefit in some ways from doing a more clear analysis of the tasks that we perform in making sure that they are in fact performed by the right people."

*   *   *   *   *

Harvey responds: "Hmm. Got to think that one over. Interesting idea. One of the dangers I see is that in clarifying all of the tasks that need to be performed at the agency, or even in my own department, well, it might lead to some rigidity. We might even find ourselves trying to train staff to fit the tasks instead of trying to fit the tasks to the staff. You know, there's always a tendency in every organization, even as loose an agency as this one, to try to make people fit.

"What we really ought to be aiming for is making the workplace fit the person. Look, if we try to do task analysis here and allocate tasks to each of the staff members in my department, we'd have a heck of a time. I mean, we don't have a formal organization structure here. We're really informal. If you try to design an organization chart for this department, it would look more like a bowl of spaghetti than a neat hierarchy of positions and responsibilities. If anything, we're constantly sharing tasks, reassigning them, picking up each person's load when there's a heavy burden on that person and expanding, redefining, and creating new tasks to perform. That's what makes us as dynamic as we are, and that's why we've grown so rapidly.

"Still, as I think about it, when new people come into the department, it can be awfully confusing. And sometimes we'll leave important things undone because we haven't paid enough attention to tasks that might seem less important at the moment, or that may be less popular. I'll think on it some more. Got some material for me before we get together as a task force?"

* * * * *

Ali responds: "I've got to tell you, Carl, when I first heard I was being appointed to this task force, I just didn't know how I could be helpful. I'm only the receptionist around here. But now that you've explained it to me, I do have some ideas. First of all, I have a good feel for what the other support staff at the agency are facing, the kinds of problems that they have to attend to every day. When we went through a cutback last year and consolidated the clerical staff into an agencywide pool, there was a lot of bitching. It made work so impersonal. And then there was the problem of everybody doing similar things. Some of the secretaries not only felt lost because they weren't close to their old bosses anymore, but because they were being required to do all kinds of things that they either didn't like to do or didn't know how to do well. This (task analysis) could have helped them.

"But there's something else that bothers me, too. It's not just what people do but how they relate to each other. I guess I have the reputation around here of getting along well with everyone. But some people don't get along well at all. You know, people have different styles, and there's some real resentment about two of the girls—I won't mention their names—in the pool who, I guess you would say, are lesbians. Now, don't get me wrong, and maybe I shouldn't even be saying this. I don't mean that people shouldn't have the right to be what they are. But it makes people uncomfortable. For me, this place is like a family, and I guess family members ought to take care of each other. Is this something we should be discussing in a task force, too?"

* * * * *

At first, Carl wasn't sure what to make of the apparent differences in the way in which his colleagues had reacted to the challenge before them. Systematic as he was, he had taken notes following each of the meetings. He now went over them. Four sets of issues seemed to have been presented by one or more people. One had to do with the *nature of professional practice* and the apparent difficulty that some staff members had in clarifying the tasks that were to be performed by professional staff. This seemed to be especially problematic for those who thought of practice as relatively indeterminant, involving "people changing versus people processing."

A second issue had to do with the *roles that people perform* in the agency. And there seemed to be a difference in people's minds between routine versus nonroutine tasks assigned to those roles. There were also concerns about the nature of the relationships between incumbents and different roles. Third, the nature of *people's interpersonal relationships* seemed to be an issue, particularly when people behaved in ways that violated either agency norms or the values held by some members of the staff. Finally, there seemed to be an issue that had to do with what Carl defined as *"creativity and autonomy."*

"Funny," Carl thought, "I'm beginning to think like a social worker. Maybe it's a good thing I'm an accountant and not so personally involved in these issues. Maybe I can help us arrive at some clarity." He decided to put these issues on the agenda for the first meeting of the task force.

PEOPLE CHANGING VERSUS PEOPLE PROCESSING

The core tasks—that is, those that are most central to the missions of a human service organization—are generally those that entail staff-client relationships. They help to define what the organization is in business for. From the staff's perspective, these relationships are aimed either at categorizing the client and his or her needs or at changing the client in some way. The more critical the need, or the more significant the change sought, the more important the nature of the relationship and often the more significant the demands made of the client. From the client's point of view, his or her relationship to the staff member is aimed at securing some sought-after benefit: a change in status or position, greater access to needed resources or perhaps more control over his or her circumstances.

There may even be a perceived intrinsic value built into the relationship itself, one that increases the client's sense of belonging, self-esteem, or pleasure in the social interaction with a staff member. If, however, the client perceives the nature of the relationship to be less than beneficial, even punitive, he or she may attempt to manipulate that relationship by controlling the degree of information provided, refusing to cooperate and circumventing the agency's rules or perhaps even opting out of the relationship altogether. After all, clients are people, each with their own sense of self and identity, only part of which is connected in some way to the agency. When clients are not forced to accept agency services, as might be the case when participating under a court order or seeking service out of desperation, they can resist the agency's efforts to categorize them or to change them.

Thus the agency is always limited in its ability to coerce or demand compliance. From your own experience, you know that a university may set up rules and procedures for satisfactory completion of academic requirements, but short of refusing to award a degree, it can do little to force students to comply. A physician can recommend surgery, but short of using emergency procedures cannot force the patient to accept the recommendation. In general, the more important the agency's services are to the client, and the less likely the client is to find a substitute elsewhere, the more likely the client will comply. On the other hand, the greater the need for the client's willing compliance, the more likely the agency will be to accommodate to the client's perception of appropriate demands and services.

These limitations on an agency's authority require that it establish procedures to minimize conflict in staff-client relationships, and that it increase staff control over those relationships. Sometimes this is done by appealing to common values ("We both want Susan to do better in school," or "We all agree that better relationships in the family are of central importance"), by pointing out the benefits of compliance ("If you register, we can assure you that the checks will keep coming on a monthly basis") or by threatening dire consequences for non-compliance ("If you don't register early, you may miss the opportunity to send your child to camp," or "If you miss three sessions, the rules require that I report this to the probation department"). Staff can also control the relationships through the establishment and maintenance of a set of procedures that keep the client at a certain distance, and with limited access to information ("Sorry, that's privileged information," or "It takes several sessions before you get the hang of it," or "If the time is convenient for you, we'll meet here every Tuesday at 10:15").

These client control tasks, central as they are to most agency practice, are difficult for members of helping professions to face squarely. They prefer to redefine them as "helping" rather than controlling. But when performing a task analysis, it soon becomes clear that many of the activities performed are directly related to controlling client behavior. And this may be one of the reasons why some members of the helping professions find it difficult to engage in the process. There may be some aspects of task analysis that are simply too threatening to their perceptions of themselves, and to the ideological frameworks that infuse and provide direction to their practice. This may be less so in people-processing than in people-changing situations.

People-processing activities tend to be composed of what James D. Thompson calls "long-linked technologies." The *assembly line* method might be a more familiar description. People processing includes several steps: reception, recording, labeling, routing, treating, and referral or discharge. Think about your own experience at the university. *Reception* would include all those activities that were involved in your recruitment (sending out brochures and application forms, other promotional activities including individual meetings or interviews, and so on). *Recording* would include collecting all the relevant materials on you as an applicant (including the material from your application forms, references, high school or undergraduate records, and so on). *Labeling* would include the process of categorizing applicants on the basis of strengths and weaknesses, interests, and aptitudes. *Routing* would then include sending the student applicant to the appropriate department. *Treatment* would include all of the educational programs and processes. *Referral,* or *discharge,* would include graduation, referral to higher educational opportunities, job referral or job routing, and the like. Clients and other human service organizations go through the same kind of process. Sometimes the process is handled by a number of different organizations, each responsible for one or two of these stages.

There is the danger that, in part of this process at least, the client may feel as if he or she has been turned into nothing but a piece of paper. Becoming a student or a client, in fact, requires becoming an artifact of the service organization. Regardless of its rhetoric or ideology, the organization is virtually never interested in the whole person. It is interested in those characteristics of the person that make it possible to serve the person or refer him or her elsewhere (that is, to change the person or to process the person in some way). In other words, the agency is interested first in transforming the person into a client and then helping the client deal with specific parts of the self.

Because people-processing tasks tend to deal only with certain aspects of the person or certain stages of the service process, they tend to be somewhat easier to describe in task terms. That may be why Sam felt it would be more appropriate to use task analysis to get a better handle on what different staff members did as a client was processed through the agency, so as to assure that each of the tasks was done appropriately and that staff members at different stations (on the assembly line) would know what had been done before and would be prepared to do the appropriate thing at their point of intervention. This may also be why Yolanda was not sure that task analysis was an appropriate approach to use in examining the treatment or clinical program. And it may account for Millicent's skepticism.

Clinical programs focus directly at changing or improving the client. Such improvement may include becoming better educated, cured of a disease or rehabilitated. One might distinguish such people-changing activities into categories like socialization, education or rehabilitation (that is, changing people because of some physical or moral defect). These changes often require an intensive involvement of a staff person, or an intensive relationship between the staff member and the client. It also requires that the client participate actively in the process of change.

The client has to want to be educated, to want to change, to want to overcome a drug habit and to work actively toward self-improvement. Social workers, educators, and other human service helpers use a wide variety of methods to induce the client to want these changes and to provide clients with the skills to achieve such changes. But these methods are sometimes hard to categorize. "It's not so much what we do as what happens in the relationship," Yolanda explained at one of the early task force meetings. There is a certain mystique in this process. And that mystique resists definition, although it certainly can be defined. But it requires a careful delineation of the tasks performed and an understanding of how those tasks relate to each other.

I am a professor at a school of social work. If somebody were to examine all the tasks that I perform, they might wish to group them under teaching, research and knowledge development, knowledge dissemination (including writing books like this one), and service (both to the community and to the institution by which I am employed). Taking one of those functions, teaching, we might further identify a wide variety of tasks that include lecturing, counseling, preparing course outlines, selecting library materials, grading and so on.

Because faculty members are notorious in their demands for academic freedom (what we earlier referred to as professional autonomy), they resist having their activities categorized into discrete tasks. Doing so would make it possible for others to evaluate the effectiveness of their lecturing, selection of books, grading and so on. In fact, categorizing tasks might make it possible to develop performance criteria by which faculty would evaluate themselves or be evaluated by others (including students). This would also lead to identifying weaknesses in a faculty member's performance and to developing training programs aimed at overcoming such weaknesses or improving competence. Would this be a violation of academic freedom? I think not. But I think it would be so perceived by many faculty people. Hence the resistance to task specification and the development of clear performance criteria.

Many professionals are similarly resistant, reluctant to have the very heart of what they do examined and compared to the work of others. It may be less threatening (and also less productive) to maintain a shroud of mystery. That shroud, by protecting the professional's work from scrutiny, increases the profession's authority over others. Moreover, some professionals argue that a task analysis would provide only a limited view of their professional behavior. Because students, campers, and other clients are themselves individuals with unique characteristics, needs, and behavioral patterns, the helping professional must respond to those characteristics. Thus, in every helping situation (like those alluded to by Millicent), the professional can be expected to behave somewhat differently. This is more true in intensive relationships characterized by people-changing activities than in people-processing activities (in which only part of the client is subject to review or classification).

ROLES AND RESPONSIBILITIES

The description of tasks, and their allocation to staff members performing different roles, can lead to the writing of more comprehensive and accurate job descriptions. No job description, however, is ever fully comprehensive or accurate. Organizations could not operate effectively if people did only what was contained within their job descriptions, nor could staff members operate effectively if they tried to do everything contained in their job descriptions. Yolanda was quite correct in suggesting that innovation and experimentation would suffer if, as Harvey suggests, someone tried to unscramble his "bowl of spaghetti-like" organization chart.

Under normal circumstances, Harvey's staff might not be expected to do any counseling of individual residents in group homes. Their primary functions are to establish group homes, locate them in the community, and make sure that they meet all the licensing standards. But in a crisis or emergency situation, staff may very well be called on to do crisis counseling and sometimes to locate people in group homes. In other cases they may refer a home resident to the appropriate professional service in the community. These nonroutine tasks are common to other fields of practice as well.

Within a particular agency or department, internal allocations of responsibilities may result in specially tailored task assignments that do not appear on the official job description. For example, in a

Exercise 6.1

Client Processing and Client Changing

1. In two or three paragraphs, describe a client-processing procedure at an agency with which you are familiar. Describe all the tasks that are performed in processing the client from reception through referral or discharge. Underline the action verbs.

2. Now describe a more intensive client-changing activity (teaching, family treatment or rehabilitation). Again, underline all the action verbs.

3. Which was more difficult to do? Why? If you had to interview staff members at your agency involved in either one or more of the steps in people processing, or in an intensive treatment or people-changing approach, who do you think would have a more difficult time in describing the tasks that they perform? Why?

vocational rehabilitation agency, all rehab counselors may be expected to do job counseling, case management, job finding, and job placement with clients of all types and with many kinds of disabilities. But in practice, staff members in a district office tend to specialize. One focuses more heavily on working with the sight- and hearing-impaired, while another works with paraplegics. One staff member becomes expert in job finding and job placement, especially in industrial settings, and may take on part of the caseload of another worker who may not have such expertise. In effect, what happens is that each worker performs a somewhat specialized role in relationship to his or her coworkers, regardless of what may be the stated uniform job description.

While the role reflects the functions, tasks and activities prescribed by the organization, it also includes tasks undertaken by the role occupant on his or her own initiative. This initiative may be influenced in part by the expectations held about that role by the people who interact with the role occupant. Some of those people are intended by the agency to do so. Examples include superiors, subordinates, and those with whom the person must regularly interact in the performance of his or her assigned tasks. These others can pressure a role occupant to conform to their expectations. Even clients can be influential, defining what they expect in terms of help, empathy, and responsibility. People outside the agency can also be influential if they are important to the role occupant who looks up to them, respects their judgment, and values their approval, or if they possess resources needed by the role incumbent to do his or her job. The behavior of staff members of any agency where referrals are sent provide a good example of role responses to external expectations.

A staff member's own perceptions and interpretations of what is expected for effective role performance also affects behavior. This is called a filtered process which, to a certain extent, distorts the messages being sent by others. Perhaps the proper word is not "distort." Perhaps the appropriate word is "shape." For example, your supervisor may ask you to call a client who is suffering a crisis. It's almost 5:00, closing time. After about 60 minutes of trying, you finally reach the client and offer help. But your supervisor may have intended that you call during office hours, because it is "unprofessional" to call after hours. An after-hours call might generate inappropriate expectations in the future. The apparent "double bind" is not uncommon when expectations are unclear.

"If I'm going all out for my client, it gets me into trouble," you might conclude. "Next time, I'll just follow the rules, and to hell with the client." What you might not have understood is that the supervisor was concerned about the client but had a different idea about how the professional helping role should be performed. Nevertheless, you were placed in a bind, unsure of his or her expectations, feeling damned if you do and damned if you don't. We'll get back to this point in a moment.

The people with whom a role incumbent interacts in the performance of the tasks associated with that role make up what sociologists like Robert Merton call a "role set." Each of the members of the role set performs tasks associated with his or her own roles in ways that articulate with a filtered perception of how the role should be performed. Sources of interpersonal conflict in an agency are often found in the different perceptions of the role by members of the role set. For this reason, solutions to job performance problems can often be found in an analysis of the role/role set interactions.

For example, Ali's job, that of receptionist, exists beyond the life of the role occupant. This is a major stabilizing factor for the organization. If Ali were to leave, someone else in that role, however, might attempt to modify the way the receptionist's role is performed. If the new receptionist behaved very differently from Ali, one might expect the initial response of other staff members to be to give the new role incumbent cues to appropriate behavior. Regardless of the role incumbent, however, substantial portions of the role, and the tasks associated with it, often remain unchanged. Nevertheless, individuals do perform particular roles differently from others placed in the same position. To understand this point, think about actors in a play.

Roles are generally established and defined in the script, but different actors will bring different styles, interpretations and experiences to the same role. The role will never be portrayed by two performers in exactly the same way. What one actor does with the role may also be affected by how other actors play their roles, or by how the director wants the script interpreted. Consider also a staff role previously occupied by a person who did everything he or she was told, but no more. Assume that a new person now occupies the same role but imbues it with a great deal more energy and willingness to do whatever will help the agency.

Would not the new incumbent reshape the expectations of others? Someone else in Harvey's role might perform it quite differently. Harvey, as we defined him earlier, is a climber, a builder. Someone else might be much more conservative, focusing on the managing of what is, rather than expanding it to what it might be. Although the basic job description might remain the same, the new department head might have very different ideas about appropriate tasks, dress, style and so on. As the new person settles into the job, the expectations of others are likely to change to accommodate the new incumbent's definitions.

If everyone in an agency lived up to current role expectations and made compatible role demands on others, there would be few problems in interpersonal and organizational relationships. Unfortunately, things don't happen this way. Role conflict occurs when contradictory expectations exist for role performance, and when living up to one set of expectations makes compliance with another difficult if not impossible. There are several sources of role conflict. Robert Kahn and his associates have defined these as intersender, person-role, interrole, and intrasender conflicts.

Intersender role conflicts occur when the person occupying a role is confronted with conflicting expectations from two or more significant others, creating a situation such that the fulfillment of one expectation makes if difficult or impossible to satisfy others. In any work situation, a particular role incumbent may be subject to contradictory expectations "sent" by other members of the role-set: the agency's administrative director, a person's direct supervisor, co-workers at the agency, subordinates, a union or its representatives, others outside the agency whose expectations have an impact on role performance (clients or workers at other agencies); or members in the worker's affective network (like a spouse or friends). When the expectations of one of these groups or individuals conflict with the expectations of another, an intersender role conflict exists.

A *person-role* conflict is of a somewhat different order. It occurs when expectations associated with a particular role violate the moral values, needs, or aspirations of the role incumbent. For example, Sam feels that Asian and Arab Americans should be treated in a special or different way. But other members of the staff feel that they should not be treated differently from other agency clients. Several of the agency staff members feel that task analysis may be impossible or inappropriate with regard to certain staff positions, but this conflicts with Carl's sense of order. Carl faces yet another conflict. He has never been able to integrate his jazz musician self into his professional self. He deals with this by not dealing with it, by keeping both selves discrete and separate. When a person is required to behave in ways that conflict with his or her basic sense of self, the person-role conflict can be acute. Yolanda, as we have seen, deals with this by turning her Black self off and her professional (white) self on when she reaches the agency.

Interrole conflicts occur when expectations attached to one role conflict with the expectations of the same individual when performing another role. For example, in his role as department head, Harvey must make sure that appropriate standards are maintained in the group homes that his department is required to oversee and license. This may require close monitoring and supervision of his staff. On the other hand, Harvey's style is such that he encourages the staff to be innovative and creative. If he overemphasizes his administrative role, he is likely to either alienate his subordinates or limit their autonomy. On the other hand, if he encourages them to be innovative and expansionary, their regulatory functions (and his) may suffer.

Finally, *intrasender* role conflicts occur when the expectations of a significant other are themselves contradictory or conflicting. This is the double-bind-type conflict we examined earlier. To satisfy one expectation would make it virtually impossible to satisfy another. Carl may be under such pressure at the moment. His boss wants him to develop more rational and measurable job descriptions. But at the same time, he doesn't want Carl's work to upset existing relationships within the agency. Yolanda is always under such pressure. Her husband, Reggie, wants her to be a successful social work administrator in the white world, but he also wants her to be at home when he needs her, and that means being culturally Black in her interpersonal and womanly role at home.

There are two other terms that might bear some explanation: *role ambiguity* and *role overload*. These may not lead directly to conflict, but, like conflict, they do lead to stress. Role ambiguity occurs when a person occupying a particular role receives inadequate information from others regarding role-related performance. It becomes difficult to satisfy the expectations of significant others when those expectations are not made known. Here we are not speaking about being pulled in opposite directions by unknown forces. Rather, we are speaking about inadequate knowledge about what is required. To a certain extent, Carl's assignment was ambiguous, and his boss hoped that by assembling a task force, the ambiguities might be resolved. In order to deal with the ambiguous assignment, Carl decided to consult with more knowledgeable peers about their thoughts on the assignment. Carl's effort to identify the critical issues that had been raised in those individual meetings reflected his efforts to cut through the ambiguity.

Role overload refers to a situation in which an individual is confronted with a large number of expectations and finds it difficult, if not impossible, to satisfy all of them in a given period. If someone were to ask Harvey why he works so hard, he would not likely respond by defining himself as a climber or a workaholic. Yet his evenings are often taken up with business: catching up on office work or preparing for conferences the next day. He's often on the go during the work day, even using his breakfast time to meet with staff or make hurried visits to group homes.

Many of Harvey's lunch hours are devoted to additional meetings with staff and with representatives of other organizations with whom Harvey hopes to establish interagency linkages. He also meets with people who may possess information that will lead to new grant possibilities and the expansion of the programs Harvey is responsible for. The demands on Harvey's time are often beyond those he can effectively respond to. The result is an occasional slipshod performance, particularly in areas that he feels are not critical at the moment. For example, oversight of group homes may be of secondary importance, and hurried site visits may occur only when time permits.

Now I'd like you to examine some of your own experiences in light of these concepts.

* * * * *

REVIEW AND TENTATIVE CONCLUSIONS

Getting the job done and getting along may conflict with each other. The conflict need not be debilitating, however, especially if roles and the tasks assigned to those roles are clearly understood, and as long as consensus exists among the key parties on how a role should be performed.

(1) People, like other resources, are important assets to any agency. Like other assets, they can be managed. But unlike other assets, they also manage themselves and their relationships, and to a certain extent are managed by those relationships.

Exercise 6.2

Identifying Sources of Conflict and Ambiguity

1. In the boxes below you will find the key terms we have just analyzed together. For each one, describe a situation of role conflict, role ambiguity or role overload which you or someone else you are familiar with has experienced or is currently experiencing.

   a. intersender role conflict

   b. person-role conflict

   c. interrole conflict

   d. intrasender conflict

   e. role ambiguity

   f. role overload

2. There are several approaches that might be used in resolving role conflicts, ambiguity or overload. These include: (1) clarification of ambiguity; (2) conformity to one or another of the conflicting expectations; (3) performing at some level of compromised behavior which represents an attempt to conform to more than a single expectation; and (4) avoidance of conforming to any but one's own internal expectations. Using this scheme, select one or two of the problem situations you described above and spell out how you might resolve the problem. Would this approach also work for the other problem situations? Why or why not?

(2) Task analysis is one approach to defining who does what to whom or to what, with what tools (how), for what purpose, and under whose directions or what specifications. Tasks are the smallest unit of work one can define. Once tasks are described, it becomes possible to specify both qualifications for their performance and criteria for evaluating that performance.

(3) Some human service tasks may be more difficult to define than others. These tend to be associated with intensive client-staff interactions, such as tasks associated with people changing (education and treatment). Others, those related to people processing, can be defined more concretely, much as one might define assembly line tasks.

(4) The tasks described tend to be related to specific roles performed by agency staff. But the ways in which such roles are performed is subject to the interpretations of the role performer and the significant others in his or her role set.

(5) When such expectations are either unclear, contradictory or excessive, several possibilities exist: role conflict (expressed in intersender, person-role, interrole, and intrasender conflicts), role ambiguity; or role overload. These can be resolved through clarification, conformity, compromise, avoidance or refusal to accommodate.

Once again, it's your turn to add conclusions from this chapter.

(6)

(7)

(8)

(9)

.

(10)

REFERENCES

Austin, Michael J. (1981). *Supervisory management for the human services* (esp. Chapter 4, Appendix A). Englewood Cliffs, NJ: Prentice-Hall.

Debloois, Michael, & Melton, Raymond C. (1974). *Functional task analysis: The training module.* Tallahassee: Florida Department of Education.

Epstein, Irwin. (1970). Professional role orientation and conflict strategies. *Social Work, 15,* October.

Fine, Sydney, & Wiley, Wretha W. (1971). *An introduction to functional job analysis.* Kalamazoo, MI: W. E. Upjohn Institute for Employment Research.

Gouldner, Alvin. (1959). Organizational analysis. In Alvin Gouldner & Robert K. Merton et al. (Eds.), *Society today.* New York: Basic Books.

Hall, Donald T. (1972). A model of coping with role conflict: The role behavior of college educated women. *Administrative Science Quarterly, 17.*

Hasenfeld, Yeheskel. (1972). People processing organizations: An exchange approach. *American Sociological Review, 37,* June.

Hasenfeld, Yeheskel, & English, Richard A. (1974). *Human service organizations.* Ann Arbor: University of Michigan Press.

Kahn, Robert L., et al. (1969). *Organizational stress: Studies in role conflict and ambiguity.* New York: John Wiley.

Katz, Donald, & Kahn, Robert. (1966). *The social psychology of organizations.* New York: John Wiley.

Kennan, A., & Newton, T. J. (1984). Frustrations in organizations: Relationship to role stress, climate and psychological strain. *Journal of Occupational Psychology, 57.*

Lauffer, Armand (1982). *Assessment tools for practitioners, managers and trainers* (esp. Chapter 3). Beverly Hills, CA: Sage.

Lauffer, Armand. (1984). *Understanding your social agency* (2nd Ed.). Beverly Hills, CA: Sage.

Lewis, M. (1980). Surprise and sense-making: What newcomers experience in entering unfamiliar organizational settings. *Administrative Science Quarterly,* June.

Merton, Robert. (1957). *Social theory and social structure.* New York: Free Press.

Mossholder, Kevin, et al. (1981). Role perceptions, satisfaction and performance. *Organizational Behavior and Human Performance,* October.

Patten, Thomas H., Jr. (1977). Job evaluation and job enlargement: A collision course? *Human Resource Management,* Winter.

Ritzer, George, & Trice, Harrison M. (1969). *An occupation in conflict: A study of the personnel manager.* Ithaca, NY: Cornell University Press.

Thompson, James D. (1967). *Organizations in action.* New York: McGraw-Hill.

Thompson, James D., Carlson, R. O., & Avery, R. W. Occupations, personnel and careers. *Education Administrative Quarterly,* Winter.

Vinter, Robert D. (1963). Analysis of treatment organizations. *Social Work, 8,* July.

Zander, Alvin F., Cohen, A. R., & Stotland, E. (1957). *Role relations in the mental health professions.* Ann Arbor: University of Michigan Press.

EPILOGUE

Epilogues are sometimes found at the end of a novel or play, rarely in a professional book. But because there was a certain amount of drama involved in the relations between the staff members discussed in this volume, and between them and the work setting, I thought you might like to know what happened to each person.

* * * * *

Harvey Marcus got the grant he applied for in Chapter 1, and two more in the next two years. Both he and Millicent were considered for the job of associate executive director when that position became vacant; Harvey didn't get it. At the time, expansion possibilities for his own department were becoming increasingly limited. So when an opportunity for a top-level administrative position opened up in the state department of social services, Harvey, with some reluctance, left the All-Families Service Center. Two of his subordinates left with him.

A third subordinate became department head for the community placement and group homes program. She put greater emphasis on procedures than Harvey and less on promotions. The department was now more carefully managed, with attention given to certification and oversight. But some of the excitement of the old days under Harvey's leadership left with him. Within a couple of years, other staff members either moved into different positions within the agency or left to take jobs elsewhere.

* * * * *

Yolanda Stephenson continued to perform professionally and competently. In a multiracial setting, conflicts that affected both her professional and her personal life were not so easily resolved. A year after the incidents recorded in this book took place, Yolanda and Reggie had a child, a girl. Being a mother created some additional role conflicts, but the rewards were well worth the strains.

Her entire career, she realized, was an exercise in overcoming strains and stereotypes. Both Blacks and women in America are expected to play subservient, supportive roles. They're not expected to be in leadership positions, or in positions of providing guidance and direction to whites (whether they be clients or subordinates at work). She was prepared to accept the contradictions and to deal with them throughout her professional life. Her daughter, she hoped, would grow up in a different America.

* * * * *

Carl Farrell continued to chair the task force. After some initial resistance, the other members began to identify the benefits of task analysis and job redesign. Their work, in fact, led to job restructuring. Following her maternity leave, for example, Yolanda returned on a half-time basis, sharing her job with another staff member. Task analysis led to a number of other changes besides job sharing: flextime arrangements and the development of temporary teams that cut across departmental levels for dealing with specific issues important to the agency.

For Carl, this success at working with a team of other staff members gave him an entirely new outlook on his work and his position in the agency. "For the first time, I began feeling like I was an integral part of the team. It feels good." He continued playing jazz in the evenings but found that work was increasingly becoming more jazzy. That is, there were all kinds of opportunities for "improvising and orchestrating," as he put it.

When the task force's work was completed, Bill Clapman asked Carl if he would be willing to continue to supervise the accounting department and also take on a new role as the agency's personnel director. "At last I'm a social worker," Carl laughed to himself. "I'll do it if we give Mary Jo a permanent job as my assistant." Mary Jo had stayed on at the agency after completing her field placement for the year that the task force was doing its work. For her, the new position meant not only security but an opportunity to continue helping to shape programs and services by devoting her efforts to improving the quality of work and work life at the agency.

* * * * *

Sam Mansouri never did get to hire the paraprofessionals for whom he had advocated. The opposition to the idea was just too strong. Paraprofessionals did not fit the agency's ideological climate, even though he felt there was a significant contribution they might make, particularly in his own department. Nevertheless, Sam found other ways to achieve the same objectives.

He and his staff devoted a considerable amount of energy to the development of self-help groups among the Vietnamese and Chaldean populations served by the New Americans Project. In fact, Sam was able to negotiate with the federal government for the responsibility of allocating funds from his grant to these groups. In turn, they were able to hire people from among their own populations to manage a variety of self-help activities. They received much technical assistance and consultation from Sam's staff.

* * * * *

Alberta Schmid's work on the task force opened up all kinds of new opportunities for her. At first, the gratification of working with professionals on the staff, and the increase in self-esteem that this brought her, led her to consider leaving the agency to earn a bachelor's degree in social work. But about that time, the American Federation of State, County and Municipal Employees began to organize the clerical staff at the Center.

Ali's knowledge of the tasks performed by different staff members, and of the structure of the agency, resulted in her being sought out by the union organizer. And her good relationship with the clerical staff led to her election as shop steward. Getting the professional degree was placed on the back burner. "It's something I might do someday," she told her father. "But not now, there's just too much to do at work."

* * * * *

Millicent Kapinski accepted the offer to become the agency's associate administrative director, albeit with some reluctance. Being an administrator didn't quite fit her own self-image, but the respect she gained from others, and the opportunities the new position offered her to help give direction to the agency's programs in areas that complemented her own critical consciousness, made up for some of the satisfaction she had derived from interacting directly with clients and others in the community.

* * * * *

That's their story. What about yours?

ABOUT THE AUTHOR

ARMAND LAUFFER is Professor of Social Work at the University of Michigan, where he teaches courses in administration, staff development, and community planning. He received his doctorate at Brandeis University and has spent several years on the faculties of the Hebrew University and Haifa University in Israel as a visiting professor.

Co-Editor of the Sage Human Service Guides, Lauffer has written a number of other professional books.

For Sage:
Understanding Your Social Agency (2nd Edition), 1985
Grantsmanship and Fundraising, 1984
Assessment Tools, 1982
Getting the Resources You Need, 1982
Health Needs of Children (with Roger Manela), 1979
Resources for Child Placement, 1979
Volunteers (with Sarah Gorodezky), 1977
Understanding Your Social Agency (1st Edition, with Lynn Nybell, Carla Overberger, Beth Reed, and Lawrence Zeff), 1977
Grantsmanship (1st Edition), 1977

Other books in print:
Strategic Marketing for Not-for-Profit Organizations, 1984
Community Organization for the 1980s (ed., with Edward Newman), 1982
Doing Continuing Education and Staff Development, 1978
Social Planning at the Community Level, 1978

The Practice of Continuing Education in the Human Services, 1977
The Aim of the Game, 1973
Community Organizers and Social Planners (with Joan L. Ecklein),
   1971